新能源应用技术系列教材编审委员会

主　任：狄建雄

副主任：（按拼音排序）

　　　　成建生　金文兵　姚庆文　朱旭平

委　员：（按拼音排序）

　　　　成建生　狄建雄　韩迎辉　蒋正炎　金文兵
　　　　李金钟　刘洪恩　刘晓艳　刘艳云　刘　颖
　　　　夏敏磊　夏庆观　姚庆文　张楼英　张素贞
　　　　朱旭平

新能源应用技术系列教材

新能源专业英语

(New Energy in English)

张素贞　刘晓艳　主编

化学工业出版社

·北京·

本书对太阳能、风能、地热能、海洋能、生物质能和核聚变能等新能源作了简要介绍，同时引用部分国内外专业研究报告及文章，对一些主流新能源应用（如光伏发电、风力发电等）的最新产品、最新技术、国内外行业发展现状及形势作了一定阐述，最大限度地让读者了解新能源的相关知识，同时能够轻松地学习相关行业英语。

　　本书可作为高职高专院校新能源专业的教材，也可作为从事新能源尤其是太阳能光伏发电、风力发电、风光互补等专业学习和研究的人员提高其专业英语水平的参考用书。

图书在版编目（CIP）数据

新能源专业英语（New Energy in English）/张素贞，刘晓艳主编. —北京：化学工业出版社，2014.8（2025.1重印）
新能源应用技术系列教材
ISBN 978-7-122-21145-3

Ⅰ.①新⋯　Ⅱ.①张⋯②刘⋯　Ⅲ.①新能源-英语-教材
Ⅳ.①H31

中国版本图书馆 CIP 数据核字（2014）第 142471 号

责任编辑：张建茹　　　　　　　　　　　文字编辑：刘砚哲
责任校对：边　涛　　　　　　　　　　　装帧设计：尹琳琳

出版发行：化学工业出版社（北京市东城区青年湖南街13号　邮政编码100011）
印　　装：北京虎彩文化传播有限公司
787mm×1092mm　1/16　印张10¼　字数234千字　2025年1月北京第1版第8次印刷

购书咨询：010-64518888　　　　　　　　售后服务：010-64518899
网　　址：http://www.cip.com.cn
凡购买本书，如有缺损质量问题，本社销售中心负责调换。

定　　价：28.00元　　　　　　　　　　　　　　　　　　　　　　　版权所有　违者必究

序

根据《国家战略性新兴产业发展规划》和国家"十二五"先进能源技术领域战略，国家出台了一系列扶持新能源产业发展的政策，在国家产业政策的引导和支持下，中国新能源产业呈现出快速发展的态势，推动了新能源产业规模化发展。新能源产业发展的速度和规模取决于新能源技术的发展，特别是核心技术的突破与进步，中国新能源增量在多个领域位居世界前列，部分新能源关键技术获得突破。中国风能与光伏产业具有较强的国际竞争力。目前中国风电产业链已逐步形成，并呈现出向产业链上游延伸、向垂直一体化发展的趋势。风电零部件制造业逐步成熟，已经有一套比较健全的风机制造供应链，市场整机设备的国产化率已经达到 70%～80%的水平。光伏产业成熟度在不断提高，中国光伏产业目前已形成包括太阳能电池制造、光伏组件封装等在内的完备的产业链体系。光伏制造业规模较大，具有一定的技术和成本优势，国内光伏市场正在逐步启动，国外市场占有率稳居世界前列。新能源产业具有很大的发展前景和空间。

近年来国内 20 多家开设新能源应用技术专业的高职院校组成新能源专业建设协作组，与行业企业一起加强合作与交流，走访 40 多家光伏、风电企业，根据企业需求进行新能源专业设置和订单培养，与企业共同开发新能源应用技术人才培养方案、课程和实训基地建设方案，加快推进学校专业建设对接风电和光伏产业，人才培养目标对接企业岗位，实训设施对接企业生产实际，促进校企信息互通、人才融通，加强校企各项资源共享、交流与合作。在此基础上成立了新能源应用技术系列教材编委会。

新能源应用技术系列教材主要包括光伏和风电技术应用，涉及到光电子材料与器件、动力、机械、电气、电力电子、自动化等多个专业学科领域，具有技术性、工程性和实践性。为解决当前高职新能源应用技术专业教材匮乏，新能源专业建设协作委员会与化学工业出版社联合策划、组织编写了新能源应用技术系列教材。本系列教材从主编和主审的遴选到编写大纲，都是经教材编委会专家反复研讨确定的。在教材编写中，内容紧扣新能源行业和企业工程实际，以新能源技术人才培养为目标，重在提高专业工程实践能力，尽可能吸收企业新技术、新工艺和案例，并以教学项目、任务为载体，按照基础、应用到综合的思路进行编写，循序渐进，努力突出高职教材的特点。本系列教材取材新颖实用，层次清晰、结构合理；内容精练，具有易于学习、理解、教学、应用的特点。

本系列教材适合高等职业学校、高等专科学校和成人高校等新能源专业教育的需要，也可作为企业员工的培训教材。

教材编写过程中得到社会各界的关心和支持，在此一并表示感谢。

教材编审委员会
2013 年 5 月

前　言

　　新能源又称非常规能源，是指传统能源之外的、刚开始开发利用或正在积极研究、有待推广的能源，如太阳能、地热能、风能、海洋能、生物质能和核聚变能等。随着煤炭、石油及天然气这些常规能源的有限性以及环境问题的日益突出，以环保和可再生为特质的新能源越来越得到各国的重视。在中国可以形成产业的新能源主要包括水能（主要指小型水电站）、风能、生物质能、太阳能、地热能等，都是可循环利用的清洁能源。新能源既具有可再生、不含碳或含碳量少、对环境影响小等优点，同时又存在能源密度低、间断式供应、波动性大、开发成本高等缺点。其产业的发展既是环境治理和生态保护的重要措施，也是满足人类社会可持续发展需要的最好能源选择。英语作为一种重要的全球化的交流工具，发挥着重要的作用。学好新能源专业英语是学生、学者和工程技术人员获取相关信息、了解产业发展动态、学习专业先进技术、进行学术交流的基本前提。为此编写本书，希望能对从事新能源尤其是太阳能光伏、风力发电、风光互补等专业学习和研究的人员提高其专业英语水平有所帮助。

　　本书每一章均由若干个单元组成，每个单元由一篇课文和阅读材料组成，其中阅读部分的内容一般对课文内容提供背景知识或者是课文的续篇和补充材料，从而达到拓宽课文内容的目的。本书分为7章，包括阅读材料在内共54篇课文，其中第Ⅰ部分内容针对传统能源存在的问题，介绍常见新能源的优点及类型；第Ⅱ部分系统介绍了光伏发电的概念、原理与类型；第Ⅲ部分介绍光伏发电在生产生活中的应用；第Ⅳ部分介绍风力发电；第Ⅴ部分介绍除光伏、风电外其他一些常用新能源；第Ⅵ部分是新能源最新产品介绍；第Ⅶ部分则是技术篇，介绍新能源产业发展的最新技术。

　　本书以提高学生专业英语阅读能力、拓展和深化学生对新能源技术的认知、培养学生应用能力为主要目的，具有以下特色。

　　① 在新能源产品和技术介绍中，倾向简单易懂、新颖有趣的课文，避免过于复杂难懂的材料，力求展现的内容清楚、准确、简练。

　　② 本书所选的课文全部来自原版英文教材和著作、公司和个人的科技报告及专业期刊，文章内容全面，几乎包含了新能源所有的能源种类，同时又突出光伏、风电、风光互补等重点能源的技术和应用。

　　③ 本书所选文章专业词汇丰富，在形式上注重图文并茂，疑难句有注释，既可作为新能源专业的英语教科书，又可用于自学。

　　本书由张素贞、刘晓艳主编并负责全书的编写，张素贞统稿。同时本书在编写过程中参阅和利用了国内外相关文献资料，充实和丰富了本书的内容。南京康尼科技实业有限公司高级工程师夏庆观以及成建生、张楼英、韩迎辉、于建明、刘乔等老师对本书的出版也给予了一定的支持，在此一并表示感谢。新能源技术涉及面广、发展迅速，由于本书编者水平有限，书中难免有不足和疏漏之处，恳请各位专家、同仁和广大读者批评指正。

编　者

2014 年 6 月

Contents

Part Ⅰ　Overview ··· 1
　Unit 1 ··· 1
　　A. Text　Energy Source ··· 1
　　B. Reading　Renewable Energy Resources ··· 4
　Unit 2 ··· 8
　　A. Text　Solar Energy ·· 8
　　B. Reading　Green Energy to Create 20 Million Jobs By 2030: UN ······················ 11

Part Ⅱ　PV Systems ··· 13
　Unit 1 ··· 13
　　A. Text　Overview of Photovoltaic Systems ··· 13
　　B. Reading　China's Energy Conditions ··· 16
　Unit 2 ··· 18
　　A. Text　Stand-Alone Systems ·· 18
　　B. Reading　Better Solar Energy Systems: More Heat, More Light ······················· 22
　Unit 3 ··· 24
　　A. Text　Grid-Connected Systems ·· 24
　　B. Reading　Photovoltaic Module ··· 27
　Unit 4 ··· 30
　　A. Text　PV Concentrator Systems ··· 30
　　B. Reading　Solar Tracker ·· 32
　Unit 5 ··· 35
　　A. Text　System Operation and Performance Parameters ····································· 35
　　B. Reading　Inverter ·· 37

Part Ⅲ　Implementation of PV Systems ·· 41
　Unit 1 ··· 41
　　A. Text　Implementing PV Systems ··· 41
　　B. Reading　Solar Off-Grid Development Trends ··· 43
　Unit 2 ··· 47
　　A. Text　New Energy Automobile ··· 47
　　B. Reading　New Energy Vehicles ··· 49
　Unit 3 ··· 52
　　A. Text　Building-Integrated Photovoltaic ··· 52
　　B. Reading　Power Station on Desert ·· 55

Part Ⅳ　Wind Power ··· 58
　Unit 1 ··· 58
　　A. Text　Applications and Wind Industry ·· 58
　　B. Reading　Wind Industry, 2000~2010 ··· 60

Unit 2 62
  A. Text   Description of the System 62
  B. Reading   Small Wind Turbines 65
Unit 3 68
  A. Text   Power Electronic Solutions in Wind Farms 68
  B. Reading   Design of Wind Turbines 71
Unit 4 73
  A. Text   Water Pumping 73
  B. Reading   Wind Chargers 76

Part V   Other New Energy 79
Unit 1 79
  A. Text   First Nuclear Power Plants 79
  B. Reading   Safety 82
Unit 2 84
  A. Text   Biomass for Renewable Energy and Fuels 84
  B. Reading   Processes of Biomass Conversion Technologies 88
Unit 3 90
  A. Text   Tidal Energy 90
  B. Reading   Utilizing Electric Energy from Tidal Power Plants 93
Unit 4 95
  A. Text   Geothermal Energy—A Quick Look 95
  B. Reading   10 Reasons Why We Should Use Geothermal Energy 98
Unit 5 101
  A. Text   Hydro Power—Time to Dive In 101
  B. Reading   Ocean Currents—Harnessing the Power 105

Part VI   New Application 108
Unit 1 108
  A. Text   A Solar Powered Ship. Wow! 108
  B. Reading   Solar Mobile Charging Stations—Thanks to Super Storm Sandy! 111
Unit 2 113
  A. Text   Introduction of Endurance's New Products 113
  B. Reading   Hybrid Towers Prevail! 116
Unit 3 119
  A. Text   Wind-Solar Hybrid Power Station 119
  B. Reading   Demonstration Project Application of Scenery Complementary 122
Unit 4 125
  A. Text   WD Series Biomass Burners 125
  B. Reading   What Chevron Is Doing for Geothermal Energy? 128

Part VII   New Technology 131
Unit 1 131
  A. Text   The Demise of Solar Silicon Crystals? 131
  B. Reading   Solar Mobile Device Chargers—Welcome to the 21st Century! 134
Unit 2 137

A. Text   Wind Power—The Basics ··· 137
  B. Reading   Commercial Wind Power—An Introduction ··· 140
Unit 3 ··· 142
  A. Text   Scenery Complementary LED Street Lamp Lighting System ····················· 142
  B. Reading   Solar Powered Cars ··· 145
Unit 4 ··· 148
  A. Text   Pros and Cons of CHP ·· 148
  B. Reading   Geothermal Place in the U. S. Power Grid ··· 151
References ·· 154

Part I Overview

Unit 1

A. Text

Energy Source

Energy means the power which does work and drives machines.

All living things (including humans) rely on the sun as a source of energy. Coal, petroleum, and natural gas are energy sources available today because organisms in the past captured sunlight energy and stored it in the complex organic molecules that made up their bodies, which were then compressed and concentrated.

With the development of society, a large of energy sources have been used, such as coal, petroleum, natural gas, geothermal energy, nuclear fission power, nuclear fusion power, solar energy, and Hydrogen gas. However, under the circumstances, the quantity of energy source is limited. Unlimited usage of energy source results in energy crisis.

At present, most of the energy consumed by humans is produced from fossil fuels. The greatest recoverable fossil is in the form of coal and lignite. Although world coal resources are enormous and potentially can fill energy needs for a century or two, their utilization is limited by environmental disruption from mining and emissions of carbon dioxide and sulfur dioxide. These would become intolerable long before coal resources were exhausted.

Only a small percentage of coal and lignite has been utilized to date, whereas much of the recoverable petroleum and natural gas has already been consumed. Petroleum has several characteristics that make it superior to coal as a source of energy. Its extraction causes less environmental damage than does coal mining. It is a more concentrated source of energy than coal, and it burns with less pollution, and it can be moved easily through pipes. These characteristics make it an ideal fuel for automobiles.

Since the first "energy crisis" of 1973~1974, some concrete actions have even taken place. However, the several-fold increase in crude oil prices since 1973 has extracted a toll. In the U. S. and other industrialized nations, the economy has been plagued by inflation, recession, unemployment, and obsolescence of industrial equipment. The economies of some petroleum-deficient developing countries have been devastated by energy prices.

Energy crisis was accompanied by worldwide shortages of some foods and minerals, followed in some cases by surpluses, such as the surplus wheat resulting from increased planting and a copper surplus resulting from the efforts of copper-producing nations to acquire foreign currency by copper export.

As known to all, the availability and cost of energy has become dominant factors in society today. Obviously, solving the "energy crisis" makes good sense. Many schemes have been proposed for conserving present energy resources and for developing new ones. It is always possible to use less energy in any process. Therefore, energy engineer is created and developed. The first goal of energy engineer is to determine the methods by which energy utilization is reduced but the output remains the same or even increases. The second goal is to determine which methods of using less energy are cost effective.

Meanwhile, looking for ideal energy sources is also very important to solve energy crisis. The recipe for an ideal energy source calls for one that is unlimited in supply, widely available, and inexpensive; it should not add to the earth's total heat burden or produce chemical air and water pollutants. Solar energy fulfills all of these criteria. Solar energy does not add excess heat to that which must be radiated from the earth. On a global basis, utilization of only a small fraction of solar energy reaching the earth could provide for all energy needs.

New Words and Expressions

petroleum [pi'trəuliəm]	n. 石油
molecule ['mɔlikju:l]	n. [化学] 分子;微小颗粒,微粒
utilized	adj. 被利用的
organism ['ɔ:g(ə)niz(ə)m]	n. 有机体;生物体;微生物
fission ['fiʃ(ə)n]	n. 裂变;分裂;分体;分裂生殖法
potentially [pə'tenʃəli]	adv. 可能地,潜在地
dioxide [dai'ɔksaid]	n. 二氧化物
obsolescence [ˌɔbsəu'lesəns]	n. [生物] 退化;荒废
fulfill [ful'fil]	vt. 履行;实现;满足;使结束

Technical Terms

traditional energy	传统能源
new energy	新能源
energy crisis	能源危机
fossil fuels	化石燃料
one-time energy	一次能源

Notes

1. With the development of society, a large of energy sources have been used, such as coal, petroleum, natural gas, geothermal energy, nuclear fission power, nuclear fusion power, solar energy, and Hydrogen gas.

随着社会的发展，许多能源已被使用，如煤，石油，天然气，地热能，核裂变能，核聚变能，太阳能和氢气。

2. Only a small percentage of coal and lignite has been utilized to date, whereas much of the recoverable petroleum and natural gas has already been consumed.

至今，只使用一小部分煤和褐煤，而大部分可回收石油和天然气已经被消耗掉。

3. Therefore, energy engineer is created and developed. The first goal of energy engineer is to determine the methods by which energy utilization is reduced but the output remains the same or even increases.

因此，能源工程师出现并发展起来。他的首要目标是想方设法降低能量消耗的同时，保持输出不变或增加。

4. On a global basis, utilization of only a small fraction of solar energy reaching the earth could provide for all energy needs.

在全球基础上，利用到达地球的仅一小部分太阳能来满足所有的能源需求。

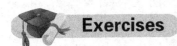

1. Put the following phrases into English:
① 温室效应 ② 可再生能源 ③ 太阳能电池
④ 风力发电系统 ⑤ 核能 ⑥ 海洋能

2. Decide whether the following statements are true or false:
① Fossil energy and nuclear are considered nonrenewable energy types.
② Solar energy is the most important renewable sources of energy, the planet with all kinds of energy are closely related.
③ There is high efficiency crystal silicon solar battery, high conversion efficiency greater than 14%.

3. Translate the following sentences:
① Energy is an important material and energy foundation of human survival and development, its plays a vital role in the development of human civilization. New energy usually refers to the new energy technologies based on new development and utilization of energy, including solar, biomass, wind, geothermal, ocean energy and hydrogen etc.

② Therefore, in the 21st century, the prospects for energy, you may have to face the depletion of oil and gas resources, the commercialization of fusion power failure during the period of temporary shortage of such people.

③ Global warming is becoming more serious. Energy saving and clean technology only can cure symptoms not cause. The only way is to find a zero emission new energy. Solar energy is the only choice to meet human development.

B. Reading

Renewable Energy Resources

1. Introduction

Some sources of energy are known as renewable energy resources. This is because, unlike non-renewable energy resources, they will not run out.

Renewable energy resources include solar energy, geothermal energy, energy from the wind or waves, energy from tides and energy from biomass.

2. Solar energy

Every year the earth receives about 3×10^{10} billion kilojoule of energy. This energy drives processes in the atmosphere that cause the wind and waves.

Some energy is absorbed by green plants and used to make food by photosynthesis. So ultimately, the sun is the source of most energy resources available to us, including fossil fuels.

Scientists also try to use the energy of the sun directly. This we call solar energy. "Solar" means "sun".

Solar energy can be used to heat fluid such as water in solar collector panels. Simple types use flat collector panels mounted on a south-facing roof or wall, each with transparent cover to admit sunlight (Figure 1-1).

Figure 1-1 Solar thermal power plants in southern California

3. Geothermal Energy

Geothermal energy (Figure 1-2) is the natural heat of the Earth's crust. The temperature at the Earth's core is over 70000℃.

Figure 1-2 Geothermal energy

The rocks, not too far below the surface, are also quite hot, perhaps at 500℃ about 1 km down.

In some areas there are "hotspots" where the temperature below the surface is higher. This is usually near where the earth's tectonic plates meet. The existence of hot springs, geysers and volcanoes points to evidence of hot rocks below the surface.

4. Wind Energy

When the Earth is irradiated by the Sun the ground absorbs some of this radiation. This heated ground warms the air above it. Hot air rises in what are called convection currents. The uneven heating of the earth's surface causes winds.

For example, if the Sun's rays fall on land and sea, the land heats up more quickly (Figure 1-3). This results in the air above the land moving upwards more quickly than that over the sea (hot air rises).

Figure 1-3 Wind energy stations

As a result the colder air over the sea will rush in to fill the gap left by the rising air.

It is processes like these that give rise to high and low pressure areas, and thus to winds.

5. Tidal Energy

Tides are caused by the gravitational pull of the Moon, and to a lesser extent the Sun, on the oceans around the world. The difference between high tide and low tide can be many meters, and the energy of the tidal movement can be used to generate electricity (Figure 1-4).

Figure 1-4   Tidal station

6. Hydroelectric Energy

Flowing rivers have kinetic energy. This energy can be collected and used. Hydroelectric power is generated by the falling of water through a turbine (Figure 1-5).

Figure 1-5   Dam

If a dam is built across the river, water can be allowed to flow in a controlled way through turbines that generate electricity.

7. Energy from Biomass

Biomass is material from living things. This could be plant material, animal material or even bacteria. Organic matter can be burned to provide heat, or fermented to produce gas.

Plant material such as wood or hay can be burned to provide heat to raise steam and so generate electricity in a power station.

Animal waste (e.g. animal slurry from a farm) can be treated to provide gases that can be burned to generate electricity. Landfill sites emit gases (mainly methane) that can also be used to provide energy. Some plant materials such as sugar cane and maize (sweet corn) can be fermented to produce alcohol. Alcohol can be used in cars as a substitute for petrol.

New Words and Expressions

tides [taid]	n. 潮汐
photosynthesis [ˌfəutə'sinθəsis]	n. 光合作用
transparent [træns'pærənt]	adj. 透明的，显然的，明晰的
crust [krʌst]	n. 外壳，硬壳
convection [kən'vekʃən]	n. 传送，对流
tectonic [tek'tɔnik]	adj. 构造的，建筑的
gravitational [ˌgrævi'teiʃənəl]	adj. 重力的
kinetic [ki'netik]	adj. （运）动的，动力（学）的
ferment [fə:'ment]	n. 酵素，发酵；v. （使）发酵，（使）激动
maize [meiz]	n. 玉米，黄色；adj. 玉米色的，黄色的
run out	紧缺

Technical Terms

organic matter	有机物。
renewable energy	可再生能源。
non-renewable energy	非可再生能源。
solar energy	太阳能；一般是指太阳光的辐射能量，在现代一般用作发电。
geothermal energy	地热能；是由地壳抽取的天然热能，这种能量来自地球内部的熔岩，并以热力形式存在，是引发火山爆发及地震的能量。
wind energy	风能；地球表面大量空气流动所产生的动能。
tidal energy	潮汐能；是指海水潮涨和潮落形成的水的势能，其利用原理和水力发电相似。潮汐能是以势能形态出现的海洋能，是指海水潮涨和潮落形成的水的势能与动能。
hydroelectric energy	水能；是一种可再生能源，水能主要用于水力发电。水力发

	电将水的势能和动能转换成电能。
energy from biomass	生物质能；就是太阳能以化学能形式贮存在生物质中的能量形式，即以生物质为载体的能量。

1. Some sources of energy are known as renewable energy resources. This is because, unlike non-renewable energy resources, they will not run out.

有些能源被称为可再生能源资源。这是因为，与非可再生能源资源不同，它们不会紧缺（即取之不尽，用之不竭）。

2. Simple types use flat collector panels mounted on a south-facing roof or wall, each with transparent cover to admit sunlight.

一种简单的使用方法是在朝南的屋顶或墙壁上安装带有透明盖板的集热板以接收阳光。

3. The difference between high tide and low tide can be many meters, and the energy of the tidal movement can be used to generate electricity.

涨潮和落潮之间的差异可以有数米，潮汐运动的能量可以用来发电。

4. If a dam is built across the river, water can be allowed to flow in a controlled way through turbines that generate electricity.

如果大坝横跨河流，可以通过涡轮控制水流方式实现发电。

5. Animal waste (e.g. animal slurry from a farm) can be treated to provide gases that can be burned to generate electricity.

可以使用动物废弃物（例如农场的动物粪便）产生可燃气体，通过燃烧发电。

Unit 2

A. Text

Solar Energy

Nonrenewable energy is obtained from sources at a rate that exceeds the rate at which the sources are replenished. Renewable energy is energy obtained from sources at a rate that is less than or equal to the rate at which the source is replenished.

In the case of solar energy, we can use only the amount of energy provided by the sun. Because the remaining lifetime of the sun is measured in millions of years, although solar energy from the sun is finite, but should be available for use by many generations of people. Solar energy is therefore considered renewable.

Solar energy is unlimited in supply, but its exploitation and utilization are limited owing to the limitation of technology and conditions.

Solar energy utilization needs an enormous amount of land, and there are economic and environmental problems related to the use of even a fraction of this amount of land for solar energy collection. Certainly, many residents of Arizona would not be pleased at having so much of the state devoted to solar collectors, and some environmental groups would protest the resultant shading of rattlesnake habitat.

Solar technologies are separated as passive and active sunlight. Active solar techniques use photovoltaic panels, pumps, and fans to convert sunlight into useful outputs. Passive solar techniques include selecting materials with favorable thermal properties, designing spaces that naturally circulate air, and referencing the position of a building to the Sun. Active solar technologies increase the supply of energy and are considered supply side technologies, while passive solar technologies reduce the need for alternate resources and are generally considered demand side technologies.

Solar power cells for the direct conversion of sunlight to electricity have been developed and are widely used for energy in space vehicles. With present technology, however, they remain too expensive for large-scale generation of electricity. Therefore, most schemes for the utilization of solar power depend upon the collection of thermal energy, followed by conversion to electrical energy. The simplest such approach involves focusing sunlight on a steam-generating boiler. Parabolic reflectors can be used to focus sunlight on pipes containing heat-transporting fluids. Selective coatings on these pipes can be used so that only a small percentage of incident energy is reradiated from the pipes.

With the installation of more heating devices and the probable development of some cheap, direct solar electrical generating capacity, it is likely that during the coming century solar energy will be providing an appreciable percentage of energy needs in areas receiving abundant.

New Words and Expressions

solar ['səulə]	n. 太阳能
replenished [ri'pleniʃt]	adj. 装满的；充满的；v. 重新装满；添加；充注精力
enormous [i'nɔːməs]	adj. 庞大的，巨大的；凶暴的，极恶的
protest ['prəutest]	vi/vt. 抗议；断言
favorable ['feivərəbl]	adj. 有利的；良好的；赞成的，赞许的；讨人喜欢的
thermal ['θɛːm(ə)l]	adj. 热的；热量的；保热的；n. 上升的热气流
vehicle ['viːk(ə)l]	n. [车辆] 车辆；工具；交通工具；运载工具；传播媒介；媒介物

Technical Terms

large-scale	大规模的，大范围的
incident energy	入射能

1. Renewable energy is energy obtained from sources at a rate that is less than or equal to the rate at which the source is replenished.

可再生能源的消耗速度小于或等于其补给速度。

2. Solar energy is unlimited in supply, but its exploitation and utilization are limited owing to the limitation of technology and conditions.

虽然太阳能是无限的,但由于技术和条件的限制,其开发利用是有限的。

3. Therefore, most schemes for the utilization of solar power depend upon the collection of thermal energy, followed by conversion to electrical energy.

因此,对于太阳能的利用方案取决于热能的收集,及转变成电能的能力。

4. Parabolic reflectors can be used to focus sunlight on pipes containing heat-transporting fluids.

抛物面反射器可将太阳光聚焦于含有热输送流体的管道上。

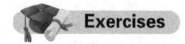

1. **Put the following phrases into English:**
   ① 辐照度　　　② 负载　　　③ 耐候性
   ④ 光电效应　　⑤ 光生伏打效应

2. **Decide whether the following statements are true or false:**
   ① The substance of this process is: photon energy into electrical energy conversion process.
   ② Solar energy is the first time, but also renewable energy.
   ③ Solar energy is not the internal or the surface of the sun sunspot continuous process of nuclear fusion reactions produce energy.
   ④ The narrow sense is limited to solar radiation of solar light thermal, photovoltaic and photochemical conversion of the directly.

3. **Translate the following sentences:**
   ① Solar energy is the first time, but also renewable energy. It is rich in resources, can use free of charge, and without transportation, without any pollution to the environment.
   ② Solar technologies are separated as passive and active sunlight. Active solar techniques use photovoltaic panels, pumps, and fans to convert sunlight into useful outputs.
   ③ Although the Earth's atmosphere solar radiation to the total energy only 22 billionths of a radiation energy, it has been as high as 173,000 TW, that is to say a second exposure to the sun's energy on Earth is equivalent to five million tons of coal.

B. Reading

Green Energy to Create 20 Million Jobs By 2030: UN

Development of alternative energy should create more than 20 million jobs around the world in coming decades as governments adopt policies to reduce greenhouse gas emissions, according to a UN report released Wednesday.

About 2.3 million people already work in green energy jobs with half of them in biofuels, said the report "Green Jobs: Towards Decent Work in a Sustainable, Low-Carbon World," commissioned and funded by the UN's Environment Program.

Creation of the jobs will depend on countries implementing and broadening policies, including capping emissions of greenhouse gases and shifting of subsidies from old energy forms to new ones, in the effort to slow global warming, it said.

The report was written before the US credit crisis reshaped Wall Street and reverberated around the world, which could slow many sectors, including alternative energy.

It said about 12 million new jobs could be created by 2030 in biofuels-related agriculture and industry.

Biofuels critics say current US ethanol, which is mostly made from corn, does little to reduce greenhouse gas emissions. But companies are racing to make cleaner, next-generation ethanol from sources including crop waste and rapidly growing non-food crops like and poplar trees.

The report said many jobs in the biofuels industry are unfair to workers. "Much of the employment on sugarcane and palm oil plantations in countries like Brazil, Colombia, Malaysia and Indonesia is marked by poor pay and dangerous working conditions." it said.

"There is also concern that large-scale biofuels production might drive large numbers of people off their land in future years." it said.

Manufacturing, installing, and maintaining solar panels should add 6.3 million jobs by 2030 while wind power should add more than 2 million jobs. Even more jobs could be created in the building, recycling, clean vehicle manufacturing sectors, the report said. (Agencies)

New Words and Expressions

alternative [ɔːlˈtəːnətiv]	adj.	可替代的
adopt [əˈdɔpt]	vt.	采纳，吸收
subsidies [ˈsʌbsidi]	n.	补贴
reverberate [riˈvəːbəreit]	vi.	波及，影响
critics [ˈkritik]	n.	批评人士
ethanol [ˈeθənɔl]	n.	乙醇
crop [krɔp]	n.	农作物

sugarcane [ˈʃʊɡəˌken]   n. 甘蔗

Technical Terms

biofuels-related   生物能源相关的
palm oil   棕榈油

Notes

1. Development of alternative energy should create more than 20 million jobs around the world in coming decades as governments adopt policies to reduce greenhouse gas emissions, according to a UN report released Wednesday.

本周三发布的一份联合国报告称，随着各国政府推行减少温室气体排放的政策，可替代能源技术的发展在未来几十年内将为世界各地创造2000多万个就业机会。

2. Biofuels critics say current US ethanol, which is mostly made from corn, does little to reduce greenhouse gas emissions.

生物能源批评人士指出，目前美国以玉米为原料生产出来的乙醇并没有对温室气体减排做出多大贡献。

3. Manufacturing, installing, and maintaining solar panels should add 6.3 million jobs by 2030 while wind power should add more than 2 million jobs.

到2030年，太阳能板的制造、安装和维修领域预计能增加630万个工作岗位，风能领域则能新增200万个工作岗位。

Part II PV Systems

Unit 1

A. Text

Overview of Photovoltaic Systems

A PV system consists of a number of interconnected components designed to accomplish a desired task, which may be to feed electricity into the main distribution grid, to pump water from a well, to power a small calculator or one of many more possible uses of solar-generated electricity. The design of the system depends on the task it must perform and the location and other site conditions under which it must operate.

There are two main system configuration—stand-alone and grid-connected. As its name implies, the stand-alone PV system operates independently of any other power supply and it usually supplies electricity to a dedicated load. It may include a storage facility (e. g. battery bank) to allow electricity to be provided during the night or at times of poor sunlight levels. Stand-alone systems are also often referred to as autonomous systems since their operation is independent of other power sources. By contrast, the grid-connected PV system operates in parallel with the conventional electricity distribution system. It can be used to feed electricity into the grid distribution system or to power loads that can also be fed from the grid.

The main components for any system are the photovoltaic array (which includes modules, wiring and mounting structure), power conditioning and control equipment, storage equipment (if required) and load equipment. It is particularly important to include the load equipment for a stand-alone system because the system design and sizing must take the load into consideration. By convention, the array components are split into the photovoltaic part (the PV modules themselves) and the balance of system (BOS) components.

As with the modules and the individual cells, the output of a PV array can be described by a current-voltage characteristic of the same basic shape and by the same parameters, short circuit current, open circuit voltage and the current and voltage at the maximum power point. In this case, the parameters now refer to the overall array. Thus the open circuit voltage will represent the sum of the voltage of all modules connected in series and the short circuit current will represent the sum of the current of all modules connected in parallel.

Since the maximum power point will vary with both sunlight level and temperature, it is usual to include control equipment to follow the maximum power point of the array, commonly known as the Maximum Power Point Tracker (MPPT). The MPPT is an electronic circuit that can control the effective load resistance that the PV array sees and thus control the point on the I-V characteristic at which the system operates.

When DC loads are to be met, it may be necessary to include a DC—DC converter to change the voltage level of the output of the array to that required for input to the load. It is also usual to include charge control circuitry where the system includes batteries, in order to control the rate of charge and prevent damage to the batteries.

New Words and Expressions

interconnect [ˌintəkəˈnekt]	vt.	使相互连接
distribution [ˌdistriˈbjuːʃən]	n.	分配、发送
autonomous [ɔːˈtɔnəməs]	adj.	自治的
payload [ˈpeiˌləud]	n.	有效载荷
reliable [riˈlaiəbl]	adj.	可靠的,可信赖的
orient [ˈɔːriənt]	vt.	使朝东,使适应,确定方向
stand-alone	n.	单机、离网
grid-connected	n.	并网
refer to	v.	查阅,提到,谈到,打听
in parallel with		与……平行,与……同时,与……并联

Technical Terms

maximum power point	最大功率点,受光照的电池在确定的伏安特性曲线上有最大功率输出的工作点,称为最大功率点,亦称最佳工作点。
system of making common electricity	并网发电系统。
system of making autonomous electricity	独立发电系统。
Island system	孤岛系统,是指不和大电网联网,只是供自己使用的光伏系统,例如只是在山里或是小岛上的光伏发电系统。
conversion efficiency	转换效率,在规定的测试条件下,最大输出电功率与辐照度,太阳电池面积的比值,以百分比表示。
solar cell array	太阳电池方阵,由若干个太阳电池组件或子方阵(组合板)在机械和电气上按一定方式组装在一起并具有固定的支撑结构

I-U-characteristic curve	电池板 I-U 特征曲线，表征太阳能电池板的输出的电压和电流的关系，代表太阳能电池的典型特征。
open circuit voltage	电池板开路电压。当电池板没有联通负载时，或者说没有电流流过时的正负极间的电压，根据 I-U 曲线就是电流为零的那个点对应的电压。

1. As its name implies, the stand-alone PV system operates independently of any other power supply and it usually supplies electricity to a dedicated load.

正如它的名称所示，独立光伏发电系统不依附于其他形式电源而独立工作，且它能向特定负载供电。

2. The main components for any system are the photovoltaic array (which includes modules, wiring and mounting structure), power conditioning and control equipment, storage equipment (if required) and load equipment.

光伏发电系统的主要组成部分是光伏阵列（它包括光伏组件，线和支撑件），功率调节器和控制设备，存储设备（根据需要而定）和负载。

3. Thus the open circuit voltage will represent the sum of the voltage of all modules connected in series and the short circuit current will represent the sum of the current of all modules connected in parallel.

因此开路电压指的是所有组件串联时电压和，而短路电流指的是所有组件并联时的电流之和。

4. The MPPT is an electronic circuit that can control the effective load resistance that the PV array sees and thus control the point on the I-V characteristic at which the system operates.

最大功率点跟踪是一种可以控制光伏阵列的有效负载电阻的电子电路，从而控制系统工作在 I-V 特性曲线上的最大功率点。

5. When DC loads are to be met, it may be necessary to include a DC-DC converter to change the voltage level of the output of the array to that required for input to the load.

当遇到 DC（直流）负载时，这就需要包括一个 DC-DC（直流-直流）变换器，改变光伏方阵输出电压值以满足负载输入的要求。

1. Put the following phrases into English：
① 功率调节器　　② 充电控制器　　③ 太阳高度角

④ 额定功率　　⑤ 环境温度　　⑥ PN 结

2. Decide whether the following statements are true or false:

① There are two main system configurations-stand-alone and grid-connected.

② For all systems, it is necessary to consider the input of energy to the system (i.e. the amount and variation of the solar radiation) and the nature of the load (i.e. the amount of electricity required and the demand profile).

③ When AC loads are to be met, it may be necessary to include a DC-AC converter.

④ The MPPT is used in any PV systems.

3. Translate the following sentences:

① Stand-alone systems are also often referred to as autonomous systems since their operation is independent of other power sources.

② By definition, because the array is not operating at maximum power point for most of the time, some of the energy that could be generated by the array is lost, so this is an operational mode that is only used when it is advantageous due to the nature of the load.

③ A graph that plots the current versus the voltage from the solar cell as the electrical load (or resistance) is increased from short circuit (no load) to open circuit (maximum voltage).

B. Reading

China's Energy Conditions

Energy is an essential material basis for human survival and development. Over the entire history of mankind, each and every significant step in the progress of human civilization has been accompanied by energy innovations and substitutions. The development and utilization of energy has enormously boosted the development of the world economy and human society.

1. Current Situation of Energy Development

Energy resources abound. China boasts fairly rich fossil energy resources, dominated by coal. The verified reserves of oil and natural gas are relatively small, while oil shale, coal-bed gas and other unconventional fossil energy resources have huge potential for exploitation. China also boasts fairly abundant renewable energy resources.

2. Strategy and Goals of Energy Development

China's energy development emphasizes thrift, cleanness and safety. Believing that development is the only way for its survival, China solves problems emerging in the process of advance through development and reform. To this end, it is applying the Scientific Outlook on Development, persevering in putting people first, changing its concept of development, making innovations in the mode of development, and improving the quality of development. It strives for high scientific and technological content, low resource consumption, minimum of environmental pollution, good economic returns, and guaranteed safety in energy development, so as to realize the coordinated and sustained development of all energy resources to the fullest possible extent.

The basic themes of China's energy strategy are giving priority to thrift, relying on domestic resources, encouraging diverse patterns of development, relying on science and technology, protecting the environment, and increasing international cooperation for mutual benefit. It strives to build a stable, economical, clean and safe energy supply system, so as to support the sustained economic and social development with sustained energy development.

New Words and Expressions

innovation [inə'veiʃ(ə)n]	n. 创新，革新；新方法
substitution [ˌsʌbsti'tju:ʃn]	n. 代替；[数] 置换；代替物
boost [bu:st]	vt. 促进；增加；支援；vi. 宣扬；偷窃；n. 推动；帮助；宣扬
boast [bəust]	vt. 夸口说，自吹自擂说；以有……而自豪
emphasizes ['emfəsaiz]	vt. 强调，着重
thrift [θrift]	n. 节俭；节约
guarantee [ˌgær(ə)n'ti:]	n. 保证；担保；vt. 保证；担保

Technical Terms

coal-bed	煤层
Scientific Outlook on Development	科学发展观
rely on	依靠，依赖

Notes

1. Over the entire history of mankind, each and every significant step in the progress of human civilization has been accompanied by energy innovations and substitutions.

纵观人类社会发展的历史，人类文明的每一次重大进步都伴随着能源的改进和更替。

2. The verified reserves of oil and natural gas are relatively small, while oil shale, coal-bed gas and other unconventional fossil energy resources have huge potential for exploitation.

已探明的石油、天然气资源储量相对不足，油页岩、煤层气等非常规化石能源储量潜力较大。

3. It strives to build a stable, economical, clean and safe energy supply system, so as to support the sustained economic and social development with sustained energy development.

坚持走科技含量高、资源消耗低、环境污染少、经济效益好、安全有保障的能源发展道路，最大程度地实现能源的全面、协调和可持续发展。

Unit 2

A. Text

Stand-Alone Systems

Stand-alone PV systems have been used to provide power for a wide range of loads in a wide range of locations. There is a variety of ways in which these systems can be classified or grouped. The International Energy Agency Photovoltaic Power Systems Programmer (IEA-PVPS) defines three categories of applications.

Service applications: includes energy services in integrated applications such as telecommunications, water pumping, remote sensing, medical equipment, parking meters, bus stops etc.

Remote buildings: such as farms, houses, hotels, education centers.

Island systems: larger systems, often PV-diesel, mostly located on islands but also in remote villages, farms or commercial premises.

Under remote buildings, there is a sub-category of basic PV system known as the Solar Home System (SHS), which has one or two modules, generally around 50W in total, providing enough energy for lighting and limited use of TV and radio. The SHS is mainly used for electrification of rural areas in developing countries.

1. Structure

The simplest PV system is known as a direct system and is shown in Figure 2-1, using the example load of a water pump (DC version). The PV array powers the load directly and there is no electricity storage facility. However, some level of power conditioning is usually needed to match the array with the load and operate the system at its optimum efficiency. This is commonly a DC-DC voltage converter in order to achieve the correct voltage for pump operation.

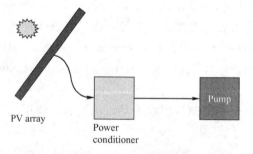

Figure 2-1 Schematic of a direct PV system, with a water pump used as an example load

The most common type of stand-alone PV system includes storage of the electricity

(Figure 2-2), usually in a bank of batteries. This allows power to be delivered whenever it is required and results in a wide range of possible applications. The system design must take account of the efficiency of storage and of the amount of energy that is needed over a 24-hour period, not just during daylight hours. Where AC loads are to be met, the system will require an inverter to convert the DC output from the PV array or battery to the AC output required by the load.

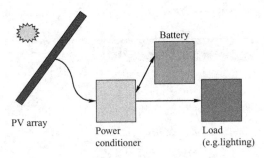

Figure 2-2 Schematic of a stand-alone PV system with storage

The third type of stand alone system includes an additional generator to provide power when the output from the PV array is insufficient and is therefore referred to as a hybrid system (Figure 2-3). It usually includes storage for meeting loads at night, but also has the possibility to use the additional generator for this purpose. This type of system is used where critical loads must be met (i.e. loads which must be kept operational, such as communications or medical equipment) and/or where there are large variations in the solar resource on a seasonal basis.

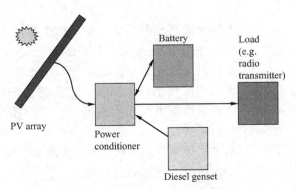

Figure 2-3 Schematic diagram of hybrid system, with this example incorporating a photovoltaic array and a diesel generator

2. Energy Storage

There are several options for the storage component of the system, including flywheels, pumped water, capacitors and conversion to fuel (e.g. hydrogen). However, the most common form is secondary (rechargeable) batteries, because they are lower cost than most of the other options and also readily available in most locations.

The most widely used battery in PV systems is the lead-acid battery, because it is the most commonly available and lowest cost. However, it is important to choose the correct type. A sealed battery is usually chosen to reduce maintenance requirements and one that can tolerate reasonably deep discharge levels should be selected.

Most systems will include a charge controller, which controls the charging rate and reduces the charging current when the battery is approaching full charge by moving to a different operating point on the array.

New Words and Expressions

module ['mɔdju:]	n.	组件
diesel ['di:zəl]	n.	柴油机
facility [fə'siliti]	n.	设备，工具
optimum ['ɔptiməm]	adj.	最适宜的
generator ['dʒenəreitə]	n.	发电机，发生器
hybrid ['haibrid]	adj.	混合的，杂种的
sealed [si:ld]	adj.	未知的，密封的
evaluate [i'væljueit]	vt.	评价，估计，求……的值
minimize ['minimaiz]	vt.	将……减到最少
equivalent [i'kwivələnt]	adj.	相等的，相当的，同意义的
category ['kætigəri]	n.	种类，范畴

Technical Terms

solar home system	太阳能家庭发电系统。指使用太阳能电池板、充电控制器、蓄电池组成的系统。安装于光能充分的区域，孤岛运行，在远离电网支配下使用，每天发电能量在几度以下。
sun collector	太阳能收集器，集热器。直接将太阳能转化为热能，使用高储热的物质诸如水或油等，之后使用热交换器使用所搜集的热量。
system efficiency	系统的效率，指光伏系统向电网传输的能量除以光照能量。
watt-peak（缩写 Wp）	是描述电池板功率的单位。
angle of inclination	倾斜角，即电池板和水平方向的夹角，0～90 度之间。
charge control	充电控制器。在电池板设备和电池之间连接。它控制并监控充电的过程。其他的功能如 MPP（最大功率点跟踪）和保护电池不过多放电而损坏。

1. Stand-alone PV systems have been used to provide power for a wide range of loads

in a wide range of locations.

独立光伏发电系统应用广泛，可用于给不同类型的负载供电。

2. Under remote buildings, there is a sub-category of basic PV system known as the Solar Home System (SHS), which has one or two modules, generally around 50Wp in total, providing enough energy for lighting and limited use of TV and radio.

在偏远地区一般采用光伏发电系统的子类型——太阳能家庭系统（SHS），它包括一个或两个组件，总功率在50W左右，提供照明及有限的电视及广播用电。

3. However, some level of power conditioning is usually needed to match the array with the load and operate the system at its optimum efficiency.

然而，为满足光伏阵列与负载匹配，需要功率调节器，使得系统工作效率最佳。

4. The system design must take account of the efficiency of storage and of the amount of energy that is needed over a 24-hour period, not just during daylight hours.

该系统的设计必须考虑存储效率和24小时（而不仅是在白天）的能量需求。

5. Most systems will include a charge controller, which controls the charging rate and reduces the charging current when the battery is approaching full charge by moving to a different operating point on the array.

大多数系统都包括一个充电控制器，用于控制充电速率，当电池将要充满电时通过改变工作点的方式来降低充电电流。

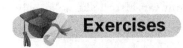

Exercises

1. Put the following phrases into English:

① 太阳高度角　　② 功率调节器　　③ 太阳能电池方阵

④ 倾斜角　　⑤ 旁路二极管

2. Decide whether the following statements are true or false:

① Some level of power conditioning is usually needed to match the array with the load and operate the system at its optimum efficiency.

② Where AC loads are to be met, the system will require an inverter to convert the DC output from the PV array or battery to the AC output required by the load.

③ All systems will include a charge controller, which controls the charging rate and reduces the charging current when the battery is approaching full charge by moving to a different operating point on the array.

④ Systems to power critical loads will be designed to have higher autonomy values.

3. Translate the following sentences:

① Compared with the single solar and wind power energy, The Wind-PV-Diesel-Battery hybrid power system which based on pure ac bus, has the advantages of compatible with the public grid, simplified design and operation of island grids, highest reliability due to redundant system configuration, all components add up their power in parallel operation, easy expandability and reduction of system costs and so on.

② This is defined as the number of days for which the battery must be able to provide the required amount of electricity to the load without any input from the PV array.

B. Reading

Better Solar Energy Systems: More Heat, More Light

Solar photovoltaic thermal energy systems, or PVTs, generate both heat and electricity, but until now they haven't been very good at the heat-generating part compared to a stand-alone solar thermal collector. That's because they operate at low temperatures to cool crystalline silicon solar cells, which lets the silicon generate more electricity but isn't a very efficient way to gather heat.

That's an economics problem. Good solar hot-water systems can harvest much more energy than a solar-electric system at a substantially lower cost. And it's also a real estate problem: photovoltaic cells can take up all the space on the roof, leaving little room for thermal applications.

In a pair of studies, Joshua Pearce, an associate professor of materials science and engineering, has devised a solution in the form of a better PVT made with a different kind of silicon. His research collaborators are Kunal Girotra from ThinSilicon in California and Michael Pathak and Stephen Harrison from Queen's University, Canada.

Most solar panels are made with crystalline silicon, but you can also make solar cells out of amorphous silicon, commonly known as thin-film silicon. They don't create as much electricity, but they are lighter, flexible, and cheaper. And, because they require much less silicon, they have a greener footprint. Unfortunately, thin-film silicon solar cells are vulnerable to some bad-news physics in the form of the Staebler-Wronski effect.

"That means that their efficiency drops when you expose them to light—pretty much the worst possible effect for a solar cell," Pearce explains, which is one of the reasons thin-film solar panels make up only a small fraction of the market.

However, Pearce and his team found a way to engineer around the Staebler-Wronski effect by incorporating thin-film silicon in a new type of PVT. You don't have to cool down thin-film silicon to make it work. In fact, Pearce's group discovered that by heating it to solar-thermal operating temperatures, near the boiling point of water, they could make thicker cells that largely overcame the Staebler-Wronski effect. When they applied the thin-film silicon directly to a solar thermal energy collector, they also found that by spike annealing (baking the cell once a day), they boosted the solar cell's electrical efficiency by over 10 percent.

 New Words and Expressions

harvest ['hɑːvist]　　　　　　　　n. 收获；产量；结果；vt. 收割；得到；vi. 收割庄稼

substantially [səbˈstænʃ(ə)li]	adv.	实质上；大体上；充分地
footprint [ˈfutprint]	n.	足迹；脚印
thicker [θikə]	n.	稠化剂，增稠剂；adj. 厚的；粗的；粘稠的
spike [spaik]	n.	长钉，道钉；钉鞋；细高跟；vt. 阻止；以大钉钉牢；用尖物刺穿
anneal [əˈni:l]	vt.	使退火，韧炼；锻炼；n. 退火；锻炼，磨练
boost [bu:st]	vt.	促进；增加；支援；vi. 宣扬；偷窃；n. 推动；帮助；宣扬

Technical Terms

heat-generating	发热
solar-electric system	太阳能发电
take up	拿起；开始从事；占据（时间，地方）
solar-thermal	光热

Notes

1. Solar photovoltaic thermal energy systems, or PVTs, generate both heat and electricity, but until now they haven't been very good at the heat-generating part compared to a stand-alone solar thermal collector.

太阳能光伏热能系统，也叫 PVT，能够生成热量和电能。与太阳热能单机收集器相比，传统太阳能光伏热能系统在转换热能方面效率不是很高。

2. In a pair of studies, Joshua Pearce, an associate professor of materials science and engineering, has devised a solution in the form of a better PVT made with a different kind of silicon.

在一项研究中，材料科学与工程副教授 Joshua Pearce 找到了一个解决方案：用另外一种硅制成 PVT 来解决效能问题。

3. Unfortunately, thin-film silicon solar cells are vulnerable to some bad-news physics in the form of the Staebler-Wronski effect.

不幸的是，薄膜硅太阳能电池易受 SWE 效应攻击（在光的照射下，非晶硅氢的导电性短时间内显著衰退，这种特性被称为 SWE 效应）。

4. In fact, Pearce's group discovered that by heating it to solar-thermal operating temperatures, near the boiling point of water, they could make thicker cells that largely overcame the Staebler-Wronski effect.

事实上，Pearce 团队发现，通过把薄膜硅加热到太阳热能操作温度，即临近水的沸点，可以把它制成较厚的电池，从而可以遏制 SWE 效应。

Unit 3

A. Text

Grid-Connected Systems

The grid-connected system is even simpler in concept than the stand-alone system. In its basic design, it consists of a PV array connected through an inverter to AC loads and to the grid, as shown schematically in the block diagram in Figure 2-4.

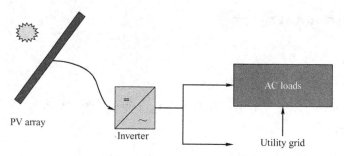

Figure 2-4 Schematic diagram of a simple grid-connected PV system.

With the exception of the PV array itself, the most important component in the grid-connected system is the inverter, which converts the DC output from the PV array into AC output, at the correct voltage and frequency, to meet the load requirement.

The input voltage depends on the design of the PV array, the output characteristics required and the inverter type. Most small grid-connected inverters operate with an input voltage range that lies somewhere between 50V minimum and 400V maximum, although there are some designed to work at both lower and higher voltages. The Maximum Power Point Tracker is usually integrated into the inverter, together with control circuitry to ensure start up of the inverter when the open circuit voltage of the array reaches a pre-defined level and close down when it falls below a pre-defined level.

Inverters for PV systems are designed to have high conversion efficiency (usually > 90% at maximum). The efficiency varies with the operating point of the inverter, but it usually reaches its maximum between 30% and 50% of rated capacity and shows only a small decrease as the power level increases. However, the efficiency generally reduces substantially at power levels below about 10% of full power.

When the inverter is grid-connected, it must be ensured that the system will not feed electricity back into the grid when there is a fault on the grid distribution system. The problem is known as islanding and safeguards are required in order to provide protection for equipment and personnel involved in the correction of the fault. Islanding is usually prevented by closing down the inverter when the supply from the grid is outside certain limits.

The grid-connected system can be used in two main applications. The grid support system usually consists of a large (300 kW — several MW) array from which all the output is fed into the local electricity grid. It is particularly useful to provide additional generation towards the end of a grid feeder where extra capacity is required, especially when the solar generation coincides with high demand (e. g. for air conditioning).

The second, and most widespread, grid connected application is the building integrated PV (BIPV) system. In this case, the modules are integrated into the roof or facade of a building and the output goes to meet local loads within the building, with any excess exported to the grid.

New Words and Expressions

inverter [in'və:tə]	n. 反用换流器，逆变器
facade [fə'sɑ:d]	n. 正面
domestic [dəu'mestik]	adj. 家庭的，国内的，主要的
tracker ['trækə]	n. 追踪者，追踪系统
significant [sig'nifikənt]	adj. 有意义的，重大的，重要的
sacrifice ['sækrifais]	n. (v.) 牺牲，献身，祭品，供奉
rectifier ['rektifaiə]	n. 整流器
solar generation	太阳能发电

Technical Terms

off-grid system	离网系统
power system model	发电系统模型
field system	野外系统
flat-roof system	平台屋顶系统
in-roof installation	镶嵌屋顶系统
peak load	最大负荷
Building-integrated PV (BIPV)	光伏建筑一体化。PV 即 Photovoltaic，BIPV 技术是将太阳能发电（光伏）产品集成到建筑上的技术。

1. With the exception of the PV array itself, the most important component in the grid-connected system is the inverter, which converts the DC output from the PV array into AC output, at the correct voltage and frequency, to meet the load requirement.

根据光伏阵列自身特点,并网系统中最重要的部件是逆变器,它将光伏阵列输出的直流电压转换成满足负载要求的电压和频率值的交流输出。

2. Most small grid-connected inverters operate with an input voltage range that lies somewhere between 50V minimum and 400V maximum, although there are some designed to work at both lower and higher voltages.

大多数的并网逆变器工作的输入电压范围在 50~400V 之间,当然也有部分是被设计为既能工作在低压又能工作在高压范围。

3. It is particularly useful to provide additional generation towards the end of a grid feeder where extra capacity is required, especially when the solar generation coincides with high demand (e.g. for air conditioning).

在需要额外容量时,电网馈线增加辅助装置显得非常有用,尤其是对太阳能发电具有高的需求场合(例如,空调)。

Exercises

1. Put the following phrases into English:

① 三相四桥臂逆变器 ② 分布式并网发电系统 ③ 孤岛检测技术
④ 电网 ⑤ 能量输出 ⑥ 温度系数

2. Decide whether the following statements are true or false:

① The grid-connected system consists of a PV array connected through an inverter to AC loads and to the grid.

② The output voltage of the inverter is chosen according to the load requirements.

③ In locations in the middle and north of Europe, the performance at low light levels can not have a significant effect on the overall system efficiency.

④ When the inverter is grid-connected, it must be ensured that the system will not feed electricity back into the grid when there is a fault on the grid distribution system.

3. Translate the following sentences:

① A new grid-connected system in the community area with photovoltaic (PV) power plant and a power storage system to utilize efficiently electric power generated by PV power plant was proposed in the community area.

② Used to describe a structure where PV replaces conventional materials and is integrated into the building. Typically, a photovoltaic array is incorporated into the roof or walls of a building. Roof tiles with integrated PV cells can now be purchased. Arrays can also be retrofitted into existing buildings; in this case they are usually fitted on top of the existing roof structure. Alternatively, an array can be located separately from the building but connected by cable to supply power for the building.

③ At present, the barrier to the large-scale application of wind and solar generation is their economic performances.

④ Wind electricity generation with surplus stored in batteries Wind electricity generation with surplus fed into 11 kW farm grid feeders.

⑤ At last, judging by the control strategy, making good use of micro control technology, the paper narrates how to develop the control system about wind/solar generation based on single chip computer.

B. Reading

Photovoltaic Module

A photovoltaic module is composed of individual PV cells. This crystalline-silicon module has an aluminium frame and glass on the front. (Shown in Figure 2-5)

Figure 2-5　Photovoltaic modules

In the field of photovoltaics, a photovoltaic module or photovoltaic panel is a packaged interconnected assembly of photovoltaic cells, also known as solar cells. An installation of photovoltaic modules or panels is known as a photovoltaic array. Photovoltaic cells typically require protection from the environment. For cost and practicality reasons a number of cells are connected electrically and packaged in a photovoltaic module, while a collection of these modules that are mechanically fastened together, wired, and designed to be a field-installable unit, sometimes with a glass covering and a frame and backing made of metal, plastic or fiberglass, are known as a photovoltaic panel or simply solar panel. A photovoltaic installation typically includes an array of photovoltaic modules or panels, an inverter, batteries (for off grid) and interconnection wiring.

1. Theory and construction

Solar Panels use thermal energy from the sun to convert solar cells into sunlight. The majority of modules use wafer-based crystalline silicon cells or a thin-film cell based on cadmium telluride or silicon. Crystalline silicon, which is commonly used in the wafer form in photovoltaic (PV) modules, is derived from silicon, a commonly used semi-conductor.

Most modules are rigid, but there are some flexible modules available, based on thin-film cells.

Electrical connections are made in series to achieve a desired output voltage and/or in parallel to provide a desired amount of current source capability.

Diodes are included to avoid overheating of cells in case of partial shading. Since cell heating reduces the operating efficiency it is desirable to minimize the heating. Very few modules incorporate any design features to decrease temperature, however installers try to provide good ventilation behind the module.

New designs of module include concentrator modules in which the light is concentrated by an array of lenses or mirrors onto an array of small cells. This allows the use of cells with a very high-cost per unit area (such as gallium arsenide) in a cost-competitive way.

2. Thin-film modules

Third generation solar cells are advanced thin-film cells. They produce high-efficiency conversion at low cost.

(1) Rigid thin-film modules:

In rigid thin film modules, the cell and the module are manufactured in the same production line.

The cell is created directly on a glass substrate or superstrate, and the electrical connections are created in situ, a so called "monolithic integration". The substrate or superstrate is laminated with an encapsulant to a front or back sheet, usually another sheet of glass.

The main cell technologies in this category are CdTe, or α-Si, or α-Si+μc-Si/Tandem or CIGS (or variant). Amorphous silicon has a sunlight conversion rate of 6%~10%.

(2) Flexible thin-film modules:

Flexible thin film cells and modules are created on the same production line by depositing the photoactive layer and other necessary layers on a flexible substrate.

If the substrate is an insulator (e.g. polyester or polyimide film) then monolithic integration can be used.

If it is a conductor then another technique for electrical connection must be used.

3. Module performance and lifetime

Module performance is generally rated under Standard Test Conditions (STC): irradiance of 1,000 W/m², solar spectrum of AM 1.5 and module temperature at 25℃.

Electrical characteristics includes nominal power (P_{max}, measured in W), open circuit voltage (V_{oc}), short circuit current (I_{sc}, measured in Amperes), maximum power voltage (V_{mpp}), maximum power current (I_{mpp}) and module efficiency (%).

In kWp, kW is kilowatt and the p means "peak" as peak performance. The "p" however does not show the peak performance, but rather the maximum output according to STC.

Crystalline silicon modules offer for 10 years the 90% of rated power output and 25 years at 80%. 2 million were sold in 2004. 4 million were sold in 2005 and 7 million were sold in 2006. In 2007 8 million were sold.

New Words and Expressions

aluminium [ˌæljuˈminjəm]	n.	铝
fiberglass [ˈfaibəglɑːs]	n.	玻璃纤维，玻璃丝
package [ˈpækidʒ]	v.	封装
cadmium [ˈkædmiəm]	n.	镉
telluride [ˈteljuraid]	n.	碲化物
substrate [ˈsʌbstreit]	n.	衬底

Technical Terms

Cadmium-Tellurid 缩写 CdTe。位于 II/VI 位的半导体，带空隙值为 1.45eV，有很好的吸收性，应用于超薄太阳能电池板，或者是连接半导体。

cell temperature 电池温度，系指太阳电池中 p-n 结的温度。

crystal silicon 晶体硅

aluminous frame 铝边框

light trapping 光的增透。在光被电池板吸收前，进入电池板的光通过反射和内表面的阻碍，光的增透对薄层电池板有着非常特别的意义，表面处理技术起着重要的作用。

photo electronics chemical solar cell 光电子化学光电池板。以电解液为基础，吸收光子，产生电子和空穴对，吸收光子是在敏感的表面层，在电解液里出现电荷流动。

1. For cost and practicality reasons a number of cells are connected electrically and packaged in a photovoltaic module, while a collection of these modules that are mechanically fastened together, wired, and designed to be a field-installable unit, sometimes with a glass covering and a frame and backing made of metal, plastic or fiberglass, are known as a photovoltaic panel or simply solar panel.

由于成本和实用性考虑，许多电池片串并联连接封装后形成光伏组件，这些组件通过机械连接组成一个固定单元，有的用玻璃覆盖，用铝及其他金属、塑料、钢化玻璃制成边框，形成光伏组件或简易太阳能电池板。

2. The cell is created directly on a glass substrate or superstrate, and the electrical connections are created in situ, a so called "monolithic integration".

直接在玻璃基底或基片上制成电池片，现场生成电气连接，这也被称为"单片集成"。

Unit 4

A. Text

PV Concentrator Systems

So far, we have discussed the two main application types for what are termed flat plate systems. In this configuration, the PV modules make up the whole surface area of the array. An alternative arrangement is to use optical elements (lenses or mirrors) to collect and concentrate the sunlight onto a much smaller cell area.

These systems are referred to as concentrator systems. They allow the use of smaller cell areas, which in turn means that the cells themselves can be more expensive without increasing system costs. Because they use high efficiency cells, the concentrator module can also have higher conversion efficiency than the flat plat module. However, it is only possible to concentrate the direct irradiation, so these systems work best in locations where clear weather conditions predominate. As such, systems have been installed in the USA, Northern Africa and parts of southern Europe but are much less attractive for more northerly locations. Only a brief overview of concentrator systems will be provided, since they currently only provide a small part of the PV market. Concentrator systems are usually used for centralized generation, feeding the output directly into the grid.

The concentration ratio is usually expressed by the factor X. For example, 100 X means that the concentration ratio is 100 and, therefore, the irradiance at the cell surface under STC would be equivalent to 100 kW/m^2 assumed all the irradiance was direct. The maximum concentration ratio achievable depends on the optical system used. The concentrator system needs to track the sun position and the higher the concentration ratio, the more accurate that tracking needs to be. Also, due to the higher irradiance levels, there will be more heating of the cell and the module design needs to address the dissipation of that heat in order to maintain efficiency and prevent damage to the cell.

There are two main designs of module. The first uses a Fresnel lens to concentrate the sunlight onto a cell positioned beneath it. The Fresnel lens is basically a collection of small prisms and because of its construction can produce higher uniformity than a conventional lens, whilst also being both thinner and cheaper to manufacture. A square Fresnel lens can achieve a maximum concentration ratio of about 70X, which can be improved by the use of secondary optics to give an added concentration stage.

The second design uses a mirror system to reflect the light onto the cell target. A circular reflective parabolic dish has a high maximum concentration ratio of about 800X and is consequently often used for solar thermal systems. The parabolic trough reflector has a much lower concentration ratio (about 30X) because they only concentrate light in one axis.

The sun tracking system needs to follow the sun to the required accuracy, with the ability to either continue to track in cloudy conditions or to be able to re-acquire the sun rapidly once the cloud has cleared. It also needs to return the array to the starting position either at the end of the day or at the beginning of the following day.

New Words and Expressions

lens ['lenz]	n. 透镜
concentrate ['kɔnsəntreit]	v. 集中，浓缩
irradiation [i‚reidi'eiʃən]	n. 放射，照射
predominate [pri'dɔmineit]	vt. 掌握，控制，支配；vi. 统治，成为主流，支配
brief [bri:f]	adj. 简短的，短暂的
prism ['prizm]	n. [物] 棱镜，[数] 棱柱
reflect [ri'flekt]	v. 反射
thermal ['θə:məl]	adj. 热的，热量的
flat plate	平板式

Technical Terms

Fresnel lens	菲涅尔透镜；用微分切割原理制成的薄板式透镜。
PV module	光伏组件，将很多的太阳能发电单元连接，然后封闭后的电池板单元。之后可以灵活串联并联。
solar concentrator	太阳聚光器。用于将阳光聚在一起的光学器件叫太阳聚光器，太阳聚光器通常有反射式、透射式、荧光式等多种。
photovoltaic concentrator module	聚光太阳电池组件。系指组成聚光太阳电池方阵的中间组合体，由聚光器、太阳电池、散热器、互连引线和壳体等组成。
reflex ion loss	反射损耗，从电池板表面反射掉的光并不能用来发电，所以要有增透层来尽量减少光的反射。

1. They allow the use of smaller cell areas, which in turn means that the cells themselves can be more expensive without increasing system costs.

它们允许采用更小的电池面积，而这又意味着，在不增加系统成本基础上，电池可以更昂贵些。

2. Concentrator systems are usually used for centralized generation, feeding the output directly into the grid.

聚光系统通常用于集中式发电的输出直接馈送到电网。

3. The Fresnel lens is basically a collection of small prisms and because of its construction can produce higher uniformity than a conventional lens, whilst also being both thinner and cheaper to manufacture.

菲涅尔透镜上是一个个小棱镜的集合，因为其构造可以比传统的透镜产生更高的均匀性，同时也更薄和制造成本更低。

4. The sun tracking system needs to follow the sun to the required accuracy, with the ability to either continue to track in cloudy conditions or to be able to re-acquire the sun rapidly once the cloud has cleared.

太阳跟踪系统需要达到一定的追日精度，不仅能够阴天条件下继续跟踪，而且能够在乌云散去时，迅速跟踪到太阳。

Exercises

1. Put the following phrases into English:
   ① 转换效率　　② 单体太阳能电池　　③ 空间电荷区
   ④ 太阳模拟器　⑤ 时间常数　　　　　⑥ 钢化玻璃

2. Decide whether the following statements are true or false:
   ① The Stand-Alone System and the Grid-Connected System are flat plate systems.
   ② The flat plate systems work best in locations where clear weather conditions predominate.
   ③ Due to the higher irradiance levels, there will be more heating of the cell and the module design needs to address the dissipation of that heat in order to maintain efficiency and prevent damage to the cell.
   ④ The sun tracking system needs to return the array to the starting position either at the end of the day or at the beginning of the following day.

3. Translate the following sentences:
   ① A two-ax automatic sun-tracking test installation is described. It has been designed, installed and used to determine the thermal performances of solar Collectors.
   ② The time interval was chosen such that the plot focuses on the Sun tracking adjustment in vertical direction.
   ③ The parabolic trough reflector has a much lower concentration ratio (about 30X) because they only concentrate light in one axis.

B. Reading

Solar Tracker

The task was to design a prototype tracking device to align solar panels optimally to the sun as it moves over the course of the day. The implementation of such a system dramatically increases the efficiency of solar panels used to power the Smart House.

Solar tracking is the process of varying the angle of solar panels and collectors to take advantage of the full amount of the sun's energy. This is done by rotating panels to be perpendicular to the sun's angle of incidence. Initial tests in industry suggest that this process can increase the efficiency of a solar power system by up to 50%. Given those gains, it is an attractive way to enhance an existing solar power system. The goal is to build a rig that will accomplish the solar tracking and realize the maximum increase in efficiency. The ultimate goal is that the project will be cost effective—that is, the gains received by increased efficiency will more than offset the one time cost of developing the rig over time. In addition to the functional goals, the Smart House set forth the other following goals for our project: it must not draw external power (self-sustaining), it must be aesthetically pleasing, and it must be weatherproof.

The design of our solar tracker consists of three components: the frame, the sensor, and the drive system. Each was carefully reviewed and tested, instituting changes and improvements along the design process. The frame for the tracker is an aluminum prismatic frame supplied by the previous solar tracking group. It utilizes an 'A-frame' design with the rotating axle in the middle. Attached to the bottom of this square channel axle is the platform which will house the main solar collecting panels. The frame itself is at an angle to direct the panels toward the sun (along with the inclination of the roof). Its rotation tracks the sun from east to west during the day.

The sensor design for the system uses two small solar panels that lie on the same plane as the collecting panels. These sensor panels have mirrors vertically attached between them so that, unless the mirror faces do not receive any sun, they are shading one of the panels, while the other is receiving full sunlight. Our sensor relies on this difference in light, which results in a large impedance difference across the panels, to drive the motor in the proper direction until again, the mirrors are not seeing any sunlight, at which point both solar panels on the sensor receive equal sunlight and no power difference is seen.

After evaluation of the previous direct drive system for the tracker, we designed a belt system that would be easier to maintain in the case of a failure. On one end of the frame is a motor that has the drive pulley attached to its output shaft. The motor rotates the drive belt which then rotates the pulley on the axle. This system is simple and easily disassembled. It is easy to interchange motors as needed for further testing and also allows for optimization of the final gear ratio for response of the tracker.

 New Words and Expressions

prototype ['prəutətaip]	n. 原型
align [ə'lain]	vi. 排列
rotate [rəu'teit]	v. (使) 旋转

incidence [ˈinsidəns]	n. 落下的方式，影响范围，[物理] 入射
aesthetically [iːsˈθetikəli]	adv. 审美地，美学观点上地
prismatic [prizˈmætik]	adj. 棱镜的
axle [ˈæksəl]	n. 轮轴，车轴
sensor [ˈsensə]	n. 传感器
belt [belt]	n. 带子，地带
assemble [əˈsembl]	vt. 集合，聚集，装配
interchange [ˌintəˈtʃeindʒ]	vt.（指两人等）交换
	v. 相互交换

Technical Terms

fill factor	填充因子
anti-reflection-coating	减反射膜
minority carrier lifetime	少子寿命
back surface field solar cell	背电场电池
substrate material	衬底材料
connection semiconductor	连接半导体，指由两个或多个化学元素组成的半导体，如镓砷，镉碲，铜铟等。
corn border	多晶硅晶体之间的边界，阻碍电荷的移动，因此单晶硅的效率总的来说比多晶硅高。

Notes

1. The task was to design a prototype tracking device to align solar panels optimally to the sun as it moves over the course of the day.

任务是设计一个新的跟踪装置，因为太阳光的方向是变化的，所以要最大限度地使太阳能电池板向着太阳。

2. The ultimate goal is that the project will be cost effective — that is, the gains received by increased efficiency will more than offset the one time cost of developing the rig over time.

其终极目标是本项目要符合成本效益，那也就是说随着时间的推移将大大降低发展跟踪机的成本。

3. Our sensor relies on this difference in light, which results in a large impedance difference across the panels, to drive the motor in the proper direction until again, the mirrors are not seeing any sunlight, at which point both solar panels on the sensor receive equal sunlight and no power difference is seen.

我们的传感器依靠这种差异继续研究，结果两种差异很大的面板都能驱动电机跟踪的方向，直到反光镜子再次得不到任何阳光，而此时双方的太阳能板对传感器能得到同等阳光。

Unit 5

A. Text

System Operation and Performance Parameters

The output of any PV system depends mainly on the sunlight conditions but can also be affected by temperature, shading and the accumulation of dirt on the modules. Table 2-1 describes the parameters that are normally used to describe the system and its performance.

Table 2-1 System performance parameters

Parameter	Definitions
Nominal array power (kWp)	The array DC power rating under Standard Test Conditions
System energy conversion efficiency (%)	The ratio of the energy output from the system to the irradiation received by the array over the same period
Array yield (kWh/kWp per day)	The daily energy output of the PV array per kWp of installed PV power
Final yield (kWh/kWp per day)	The daily energy delivered to the load per kWp of installed PV power
Reference yield (kWh/kWp per day)	The theoretically available daily energy per kWp of installed PV power
Performance ratio	The ratio of the energy actually delivered to the PV energy theoretically available, equal to the final yield divided by the reference yield

In order to calculate the parameters, it is necessary to know the measured output from the system and the irradiation in the plane of the array over the same period. When considering measured values, it is also important to know the monitoring fraction. This is the fraction of time for which data are available compared to the maximum possible for that period. It is not always possible to avoid losing some data when long term monitoring is undertaken, but if the monitoring fraction is low, then the values is unreliable.

The calculation of the nominal array power and the system yields are straightforward. The equations for system efficiency and performance ratio, PR, are as follows:

$$Efficiency = \frac{100 \times E_{AC}}{A \times I_{IP} \times N \times MF}$$

$$PR = \frac{100 \times E_{AC}}{P \times I_{IP} \times N \times MF}$$

- E_{AC} is the AC output of the PV system (kW·h)
- A is the area of the PV array (m^2)
- P is the power rating of the PV array (kW)
- I_{IP} is the daily irradiation in the plane of the array (kW·h/m^2)
- N is the number of days in the period
- MF is the monitoring fraction (value between 0 and 1)

The performance ratio gives a measure of the losses in the system. It compares the actual output with the output of a loss-less system of the same design in the same location.

Note that the PR value is not affected by module efficiency, since it compares the output achieved with an ideal system using the same components. PR values of between 0.8 and 0.9 are considered good for grid-connected systems. By contrast, the system efficiency value is determined by the efficiency of each component in the system and therefore varies considerably with system design and module efficiency. Thus the PR value is much more informative in judging the effectiveness of a system.

However, for stand-alone systems, the PR value is not as useful as a parameter as for grid-connected systems. This is because the system is not always working at the maximum power point, for example when the load is low and the battery is fully charged. Thus, the PR value not only depends on the system losses in this case, but also on the mode of operation of the system. PR values for well designed stand-alone systems can therefore be substantially lower than for grid-connected systems.

New Words and Expressions

dirt [də:t]	n.	污垢，泥土
parameter [pəˈræmitə]	n.	参数，参量
fraction [ˈfrækʃən]	n.	小部分，片断，分数
ratio [ˈreiʃiəu]	n.	比，比率
substantially [səbˈstænʃəl]	adv.	充分地
affect [əˈfekt]	vt.	影响
assessment [əˈsesmənt]	n.	估价，被估定的金额

Technical Terms

absorptions coefficient	吸收系数，吸收强度。
concentrator solar cell	浓缩电池板，借助反光镜或是透镜使阳光汇聚在电池板上，缺点是要不停地控制它的焦点一直在电池板上，因为太阳在不停地动。
concentration ratio	聚光率，聚光器接收到的阳光光通量与太阳电池接收到的光通量之比。
geometrical concentrator ratio	几何聚光率，聚光器面积与太阳电池面积之比。
kWp, peak	指的是最大的功率点，单位是千瓦，一般太阳能逆变器的功率指的就是最大功率。

1. The output of any PV system depends mainly on the sunlight conditions but can also be affected by temperature, shading and the accumulation of dirt on the modules.

光伏发电系统的输出主要取决于日照条件，但也受温度、阴影和组件积累的污垢影响。

2. It is not always possible to avoid losing some data when long term monitoring is undertaken, but if the monitoring fraction is low, then the values are unreliable.

长期监测，丢失一些数据可能难以避免，如果监测精度低，得到的值也是不可靠的。

3. The performance ratio gives a measure of the losses in the system. It compares the actual output with the output of a loss-less system of the same design in the same location.

性能比（PR）公式给出测量系统损失的方法，它是相同位置实际输出与一个无损耗的相同的设计系统输出的比值。

4. This is because the system is not always working at the maximum power point, for example when the load is low and the battery is fully charged.

这是因为该系统并不总是工作在最大功率点，例如，当负载低且电池充满电时。

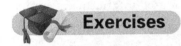

Exercises

1. Put the following phrases into English:

① 变压器　　　　② 三相电压控制器　　　③ 正面系统
④ 充电显示器　　⑤ 薄膜电池　　　　　　⑥ 发电系统模型

2. Decide whether the following statements are true or false:

① The output of any PV system only depends on the sunlight conditions.

② The PR value is affected by module efficiency.

③ However, for stand-alone systems, the PR value is not as useful as a parameter as for grid-connected systems.

④ Both the system efficiency and the performance ratio include the irradiation in the calculation and so are independent of the weather conditions, except where these affect the output.

3. Translate the following sentences:

① Note that the PR value is not affected by module efficiency, since it compares the output achieved with an ideal system using the same components.

② The yield values do not explicitly include the sunlight level received over the period, so account must be taken of whether the level was above or below average if the yield is to be used for a critical assessment of system performance.

③ The high operating temperature decreases the efficiency of PV module, and it also much lowers the maximum power voltage.

B. Reading

Inverter

1. Introduction

An inverter is an electrical device that converts direct current (DC) to alternating current (AC); the converted AC can be at any required voltage and frequency with the use of appropriate transformers, switching, and control circuits. Solid-state inverters have no moving parts and are used in a wide range of applications, from small switching power supplies in computers, to large electric utility high-voltage direct current applications that transport bulk power. Inverters are commonly used to supply AC power from DC sources such as solar panels or batteries.

There are two main types of inverter. The output of a modified sine wave inverter is similar to a square wave output except that the output goes to zero volts for a time before switching positive or negative. It is simple and low cost and is compatible with most electronic devices, except for sensitive or specialized equipment, for example certain laser printers. A pure sine wave inverter produces a nearly perfect sine wave output ($<3\%$ total harmonic distortion) that is essentially the same as utility-supplied grid power. Thus it is compatible with all AC electronic devices. This is the type used in grid-tie inverters. Its design is more complex, and costs 5 or 10 times more per unit power the electrical inverter is a high-power electronic oscillator. It is so named because early mechanical AC to DC converters were made to work in reverse, and thus were "inverted", to convert DC to AC. The inverter performs the opposite function of a rectifier.

2. Applications

(1) DC power source utilization

An inverter converts the DC electricity from sources such as batteries, solar panels, or fuel cells to AC electricity. The electricity can be at any required voltage; in particular it can operate AC equipment designed for mains operation, or rectified to produce DC at any desired voltage. Grid tie inverters can feed energy back into the distribution network because they produce alternating current with the same wave shape and frequency as supplied by the distribution system. They can also switch off automatically in the event of a blackout. Micro-inverters convert direct current from individual solar panels into alternating current for the electric grid. They are grid tie designs by default.

(2) Uninterruptible power supplies

An uninterruptible power supply (UPS) uses batteries and an inverter to supply AC power when main power is not available. When main power is restored, a rectifier supplies DC power to recharge the batteries.

(3) Induction heating

Inverters convert low frequency main AC power to a higher frequency for use in induction heating. To do this, AC power is first rectified to provide DC power. The inverter then changes the DC power to high frequency AC power.

(4) HVDC power transmission

With HVDC power transmission, AC power is rectified and high voltage DC power is transmitted to another location. At the receiving location, an inverter in a static inverter plant converts the power back to AC.

(5) Variable-frequency drives

A variable-frequency drive controls the operating speed of an AC motor by controlling the frequency and voltage of the power supplied to the motor. An inverter provides the controlled power. In most cases, the variable-frequency drive includes a rectifier so that DC power for the inverter can be provided from main AC power. Since an inverter is the key component, variable-frequency drives are sometimes called inverter drives or just inverters.

(6) Electric vehicle drives

Adjustable speed motor control inverters are currently used to power the traction motors in some electric and diesel-electric rail vehicles as well as some battery electric vehicles and hybrid electric highway vehicles such as the Toyota Prius and Fisker Karma. Various improvements in inverter technology are being developed specifically for electric vehicle applications. In vehicles with regenerative braking, the inverter also takes power from the motor (now acting as a generator) and stores it in the batteries.

(7) The general case

A transformer allows AC power to be converted to any desired voltage, but at the same frequency. Inverters, plus rectifiers for DC, can be designed to convert from any voltage, AC or DC, to any other voltage, also AC or DC, at any desired frequency. The output power can never exceed the input power, but efficiencies can be high, with a small proportion of the power dissipated as waste heat.

New Words and Expressions

bulk [bʌlk]	n. 大小，体积
similar ['similə]	adj. 相似的，类似的
negative ['negətiv]	adj. 否定的，消极的
harmonic [haːˈmɔnik]	adj. 谐波的；n. 谐波，和声，谐函数
blackout ['blækaut]	n. 灯火管制，眩晕，中断
rectifier ['rektifaiə]	n. 整流器
transformer [trænsˈfɔːmə]	n. 变压器
exceed [ikˈsiːd]	vt. 超越，胜过

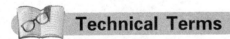

Technical Terms

uninterruptible power supply	（UPS）不间断电源。是一种含有储能装置，以逆变器为主要组成部分的恒压恒频的不间断电源。主要用于给单台计算机、计算机网络系统或其他电力电子设备提供不间断的电力供应。
harmonic distortion	谐波失真

ohmic contact   欧姆接触
standard test conditions   标准测试条件

Notes

1. An inverter is an electrical device that converts direct current (DC) to alternating current (AC); the converted AC can be at any required voltage and frequency with the use of appropriate transformers, switching, and control circuits.

逆变器是一种能将直流电转化为可变交流电的电子装置,它使用适当的变压器、开关以及控制电路实现将交流电调整到合适的电压以及频率值。

2. The electricity can be at any required voltage; in particular it can operate AC equipment designed for mains operation, or rectified to produce DC at any desired voltage.

转换后的交流电可以是任意电压值,既可以实现交流设备操作,又可滤波产生任何需要的直流电压。

3. Adjustable speed motor control inverters are currently used to power the traction motors in some electric and diesel-electric rail vehicles as well as some battery electric vehicles and hybrid electric highway vehicles such as the Toyota Prius and Fisker Karma.

调速电动机控制逆变器目前用于电力牵引方面,如一些电动和柴油电动轨道车辆以及一些电动汽车上的电机。丰田 Prius 和 Fisker Karma 混合动力电动汽车也是采用类似的调速控制逆变器。

4. Inverters, plus rectifiers for DC, can be designed to convert from any voltage, AC or DC, to any other voltage, also AC or DC, at any desired frequency.

逆变器,带直流的整流器,可以实现任何形式电压转换,交流-直流转换,电压幅值、频率可调。

Part Ⅲ Implementation of PV Systems

Unit 1

A. Text

Implementing PV Systems

In this section, we will briefly discuss some issues in relation to implementing PV systems, particularly how we might deal with output variations, how PV systems contribute environmentally and the current and future economics of PV systems.

1. Variability of Output

PV systems only provide electrical power when there is sunlight, although they operate over a wide range of light intensities (down to about the level where street lights start to turn on). They also respond almost immediately to changes in light intensity, so the output will fluctuate when, for example, clouds cross in front of the sun.

Have a mix of generation technologies with different operating periods to balance out the generation profile—for example, the wind resource is often highest overnight or in periods of poor weather from the point of view of sunlight.

It is also possible to consider modification of demand to more closely match the supply of electricity from the PV system (or any other renewable energy system). In this case, we would turn off loads that are not required when output is low and this will often have little effect on the perceived function of the device.

2. Environmental Issues

One of the main reasons to consider the widespread use of PV systems now, given that they are not yet economically competitive, is their environmental benefit, particularly in regard to greenhouse gas emissions. PV systems have no emissions in operation and are also silent, so they are one of the most environmentally benign technologies during the operating phase. That is why it is possible to mount them on buildings, very close to the occupants using the loads, without disturbance.

However, no electricity generation technology is without environmental impacts and for PV systems these occur during the manufacture of the PV modules and other components, during installation due to the transport of materials to site and during recycling or disposal. For this reason, the industry is continuously developing new techniques and processes to minimize the environmental impacts of manufacture. These impacts include waste materials produced and the energy content of both the constituent materials and the processes used.

It is also necessary to consider recycling or disposal of the system components at the end of their lifetime. How long this would be varies depending on the type of component. The PV modules are expected to last up to 30 years (or perhaps longer in some cases), whereas the inverter may only operate for 10~15 years (although the industry is addressing this aspect in their research) and batteries for perhaps 5 years.

3. Economics of PV Systems

Most renewable energy systems have, relative to conventional power generation, high initial costs and low running costs. This can make the system installation hard to finance, especially where there is little disposable income. PV system costs have reduced dramatically over the last two decades with a "learning curve" of about 80%, i.e. the costs reduce by 20% for every doubling of the market. However, PV costs still remain too high to be commercially viable without subsidy except for some specific applications in remote areas where other sources of energy are limited and expensive.

New Words and Expressions

implementation [ˌimplimenˈteiʃən]	n.	执行，应用
fluctuate [ˈflʌktjueit]	vi.	变动，波动
widespread [ˈwaidˈspred]	adj.	分布广泛的，普遍的
mount [maunt]	vt.	装上，设置，安放
disposal [disˈpəuzəl]	n.	处理，处置，支配
subsidy [ˈsʌbsidi]	n.	补助、补贴

Technical Terms

insulation strength	绝缘强度
impact strength	冲击强度
sequence number	序号
hybrid system	混合型系统
power conditioner	电力调节器；负责电力调节功能设备的统称，对蓄电池充电/放电调节的控制器，或将直流转换交流调节的换流器皆是

Notes

1. They also respond almost immediately to changes in light intensity, so the output will fluctuate when, for example, clouds cross in front of the sun.

它们也会对光强快速反应，对应的输出将会发生波动，比如，当乌云遮住太阳时。

2. Have a mix of generation technologies with different operating periods to balance out the generation profile—for example, the wind resource is often highest overnight or in periods of poor weather from the point of view of sunlight.

采用不同发电技术系统的综合，实现不同阶段采用不同的发电类型，比如，夜间或恶劣天气情况下效果相对光伏发电更好。

3. For this reason, the industry is continuously developing new techniques and processes to minimize the environmental impacts of manufacture.

出于这个原因，业界不断开发新的技术和工艺，将对环境的影响降到最低。

4. However, PV costs still remain too high to be commercially viable without subsidy except for some specific applications in remote areas where other sources of energy are limited and expensive.

然而，光伏发电成本太高，如果没有补助商业推广价值较低，除非是对于地处偏远而又能源短缺且昂贵的地区。

Exercises

1. Put the following phrases into English:
① 偏远地区　　② 风光互补发电系统　　③ 能量转换
④ 独立家庭电源系统　　⑤ 充电显示器　　⑥ 产能

2. Decide whether the following statements are true or false:
① PV systems will provide electrical power whenever there is sunlight, because they operate over a wide range of light intensities.
② We would turn off loads that are not required when output is low and this will often have little effect on the perceived function of the device.
③ Most renewable energy systems have, relative to conventional power generation, high initial costs and low running costs.

3. Translate the following sentences:
① This paper presents a utility single phase inverting system, which connects the PV system with the grid. It can get the energy from the grid when the energy of PV system is lack, and if there is surplus energy in the PV system, it can feedback the energy to the grid.
② Commercial Development Situation and Market Prospect Analysis of Jiang Su Solar PV System.
③ This paper introduces the principle of PV system and its application in the power supply of buildings-BIPV.

B. Reading

Solar Off-Grid Development Trends

With the professional needs of the people's awareness of environmental protection and outdoor sports enthusiasts, in recent years, photovoltaic applications market grew significantly. Flashlight, photovoltaic, photovoltaic cell phone chargers, photovoltaic TV, photovoltaic radios and other products has been widely welcomed.

Solar off-grid products are mainly the following forms:

1. User of solar power

(1) small power 10~100W range for soldiers and civilians living power in remote areas without electricity (Figure 3-1), such as plateaus, islands and pastoral areas, border posts, such as lighting, television, tape recorders. (2) PV water pumps (Figure 3-2): deep wells for drinking resolve areas without electricity, irrigation.

Figure 3-1   Solar lighting system

Figure 3-2   PV water pumps

2. The transport sector

such as beacon lights, traffic/railroad signals (Figure 3-3), traffic warning/marker lamps, street lamps (Figure 3-4), high-altitude obstacle lights, highway/railway wireless telephone booth unattended Road class power supply.

Figure 3-3   Solar traffic lights

Figure 3-4   Street lighting system

3. Communication/communication field

solar unattended microwave relay station (Figure 3-5), cable maintenance stations, radio/communications/paging power system; rural telephone carrier photovoltaic system, portable communication machine, soldiers, GPS powered.

Figure 3-5 Solar unattended microwave relay station

4. Petroleum, marine, meteorological fields

cathodic protection of oil pipelines and reservoirs gate solar power system (Figure 3-6), the life of the oil drilling platform and emergency power supply, marine testing equipment, meteorological/hydrological observation equipment and so on.

Figure 3-6 Oil pipeline monitoring system

5. Family lamp power

such as garden lights, portable lamps, camping lamps (Figure 3-7), light hiking, fishing lights, black lights, tapping light (Figure 3-8), energy-saving lamps and so on.

Figure 3-7 Solar portable lamp

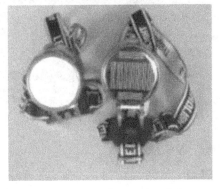

Figure 3-8 Solar tapping light

6. Other areas include

(1) matching with the car solar car/electric vehicle battery charging equipment (Figure 3-9), car air conditioning, ventilation fans, cold boxes. (2) Renewable solar hydrogen fuel cell power generation system (Figure 3-10). (3) Desalination equipment supply.

Figure 3-9 Sun light charging equipment   Figure 3-10 Solar car

New Words and Expressions

awareness [əˈweənəs]	*n.*	知道，晓得
enthusiast [inˈθjuːziæst]	*n.*	热心家，狂热者
widget [ˈwidʒit]	*n.*	小组件
pastoral [ˈpɑːstərəl]	*n.*	牧区
beacon [ˈbiːkən]	*n.*	烟火，灯塔；*v.* 照亮
cathodic [kəˈθɔdik]	*adj.*	阴极的，负极的
pipeline [ˈpaipˌlain]	*n.*	管道，传递途径
hydrological [ˌhaiˈdrɔlədʒi]	*adj.*	水文学的
ventilation [ˌventiˈleiʃən]	*n.*	通风，流通空气
desalination [diːˌsæliˈneiʃən]	*n.*	减少盐分，脱盐作用

Technical Terms

photovoltaic cell phone charger	光伏手机充电器
PV water pump	光伏水泵
beacon light	航标灯
GPS powered	GPS 供电
oil pipeline monitoring system	石油管道监控系统
energy-saving lamps	节能灯
car air conditioning	汽车空调

Notes

1. With the professional needs of the people's awareness of environmental protection

and outdoor sports enthusiasts, in recent years, photovoltaic applications market grew significantly.

随着人们的环保意识提高和一些户外运动爱好者的专业需求，近年来光伏应用产品市场增长显著。

2. Small power 10~100W range for soldiers and civilians living power in remote areas without electricity, such as plateaus, islands and pastoral areas, border posts, such as lighting, television, tape recorders.

小型电源 10~100W 不等，用于边远无电地区如高原、海岛、牧区、边防哨所等军民生活用电，如照明、电视、收录机等。

3. The transport sector: such as beacon lights, traffic/railroad signals, traffic warning marker lamps, street lamps, high-altitude obstacle lights, highway/railway wireless telephone booth unattended Road class power supply.

交通领域：如航标灯、交通/铁路信号灯、交通警示/标志灯、路灯、高空障碍灯、高速公路/铁路无线电话亭、无人值守道班供电等。

4. Petroleum, marine, meteorological fields: cathodic protection of oil pipelines and reservoirs gate solar power system, the life of the oil drilling platform and emergency power supply, marine testing equipment, meteorological/hydrological observation equipment and so on.

石油、海洋、气象领域：石油管道和水库闸门阴极保护太阳能电源系统、石油钻井平台生活及应急电源、海洋检测设备、气象/水文观测设备等。

Unit 2

A. Text

New Energy Automobile

Solar car is a car driven by solar energy. Compared with traditional heat engine-driven cars, solar car is true zero emission. Because of its environmental characteristics, solar car was advocated by many countries, solar car industry is also increasingly robust.

Since solar car without burning fossil fuels, so it will not emit harmful substances. It is estimated that if the solar car replace vehicles, each car's carbon dioxide emission can be reduced 43%~54%.

Among the domestic sales of cars, Mercedes-Benz E Class, Audi A8, A6L, A4, and some other models are equipped with a solar sunroof.

The definition of pure electric vehicles: pure electric vehicle is completely powered by a rechargeable battery.

Pure electric vehicles advantages:

① No pollution, low noise;

② Simple structure, easy maintenance;

③ High energy conversion efficiency; recovered braking energy when going downhill, improve energy efficiency;

④ Can use the grid cheap "Valley Electric" to recharge at night.

Hybrid electric vehicles (HEVs), fuel saving and environment friendly, have stolen the markets as international oil price soared up. It was reported that sales of Toyota Prius series HEVs is out of stock in international market. Grasping the opportunity, Toyota announced that it is developing a new generation of Lithium Iron Phosphate battery for HEVs with PANASONIC, which will be officially put into mass production in 2009, to strengthen its leading position in HEV market.

In June 2008, Toyota disclosed that it will invest in Australia to make HEVs, which will be Toyota's third HEV production base abroad after the U. S. A. and China. Toyota will invest in its Melbourne's factory to produce CAMRY HEVs, and it plans to eventually achieve the target of an annual production of 10,000 Vehicles.

New Words and Expressions

traditional [trəˈdiʃənəl]	adj.	传统的，惯例的
advocate [ˈædvəkeit]	vt.	提倡
robust [rəuˈbʌst]	n.	鲁棒性、稳定性
emit [iˈmit]	vt.	发出，放射
substance [ˈsʌbstəns]	n.	物质
rechargeable [riːˈtʃɑːdʒəbl]	adj.	可再充电的
efficiency [iˈfiʃənsi]	n.	效率，功效
grasp [grɑːsp]	vt.	抓住，掌握
abroad [əˈbrɔːd]	adv.	往国外

Technical Terms

carbon dioxide	二氧化碳
greenhouse effect	温室效应
hybrid electric vehicles	混合动力汽车
the pure electric vehicles	纯电动汽车
fuel cell vehicles (FCEV)	燃料电池汽车

Notes

1. Solar car is a car driven by solar energy. Compared with traditional heat engine-driven cars, solar car is true zero emission.

太阳能电动汽车是指由太阳能驱动的汽车，与传统热能驱动的汽车相比，它真正达到了零污染。

2. It is estimated that if the solar car replace vehicles, each car's carbon dioxide emission can be reduced 43%~54%.

据统计，如果用太阳能汽车替代传统汽车，那么二氧化碳的排放量将会减少43%~54%。

3. Hybrid electric vehicles (HEVs), fuel saving and environment friendly, have stolen the markets as international oil price soared up.

混合动力电动汽车（HEV），因其节约燃料、环境友好，随着国际油价飙升已迅速抢占市场。

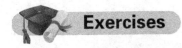

Put the following Sentences into English:

1. 新能源汽车是指采用非常规的车用燃料作为动力来源（或使用常规的车用燃料，但采用新型车载动力装置），综合车辆的动力控制和驱动方面的先进技术，形成的技术原理先进、具有新技术、新结构的汽车。

2. 目前，大规模使用石油产品的汽车，已造成了环境的严重污染，各国政府都在考虑制定更加严格的汽车尾气排放标准。因此新能源汽车必须要明显减少尾气排放的污染，甚至要达到零排放，才能被人们广泛接受。

3. 世界汽车工业竞争激烈，新能源汽车要广泛进入市场，必须在价格上占有一定的优势，这就要求车用能源售价低廉，并且使用费用低。

B. Reading

New Energy Vehicles

The main point of this report is to illustrate the reasons why New Energy Vehicles will influence Gasoline Vehicles in the future.

1. Introduction

(1) Background of New Energy Vehicles

Automobiles are popularly demanded as vehicle tool nowadays. China had accelerated the automobile industry since 1980. During the thirty years, China raised the amount of vehicle production from 100,000 to 10,000,000 each year.

Because of its convenient and comfortable, buying a domestic automobile is very hot. Along with the development of automobile industry, varied cars are produced for different consumers but customer buying criteria never change. People will consider of the consumption of gasoline of the car and the price of it. So lower price and whether save petrol become the principles when buying a car.

As a result, New Energy Vehicles are developed in 2004 (Figure 3-11), not only for driving cheaper, but also decreasing greenhouse effect. Usually we call hybrid vehicles and electric vehicles (EVs) as new energy vehicles; China is more likely to do something in

Figure 3-11　New energy vehicles

electric vehicles in the coming decades.

(2) Advantages of EVs

Electric vehicles (we call them "EVs" in this report) are propelled by an electric motor powered by rechargeable battery packs. Electric motors have several advantages over internal combustion engines (ICEs)

Such as

- Energy efficient
- Environmentally friendly
- Performance benefits
- Reduce energy dependence
- Recharge time

(3) Disadvantages of EVs

EVs are not perfect vehicles; they still have some bottleneck to breakthrough:

- Hard to breakthrough the core technology
- Prices of EVs are universally high.
- The battery has to be charged regularly. It takes about 6-8 hours to recharge completely.
- Limits on driving distance. The normal working range of battery is about 80~130 miles.
- Lack of power

2. Body

(1) National plan about New Energy Vehicles

Ministry of Industry and Information Technology (MIIT) announced recently that China will input over 100 million to support the production of New Energy Vehicles in the coming 10 years. By that time China will be the largest New Energy Vehicles producing country in the world.

(2) Policies for New Energy Vehicles from governments

As EVs have several problems to be promoted, China's government should unveil new policies especially for the high cost in order to enhance purchasing power from citizens. So from the beginning of 2009 till today, China's government and some regional government came up with a set of new policies for EVs one after another.

In December 9th 2009, Shanghai, Chongqing, Wuhan, Shenzhen and Beijing are chosen as the experimental cities which can sale new energy vehicles for personal use. The governments of Chongqing and Shenzhen have release a policy of subsidy, buyers can get a subsidy of buying EVs. The maximum of subsidy of buying new energy vehicles raise to 60,000 Yuan by Shenzhen government.

New Words and Expressions

gasoline ['gæsəli:n]	n.	汽油
raise [reiz]	vt.	升起，提高，使出现
criteria [krai'tiəriə]	n.	标准
decade ['dekeid]	n.	十年，十
propel [prəu'pel]	vt.	推进，驱使
bottleneck ['bɔtlnek]	n.	瓶颈
unveil [ˌʌn'veil]	vt.	使公诸于众，揭开
regional ['ri:dʒənəl]	adj.	整个地区的，地方的

Technical Terms

recharge time	充电时间
internal combustion engines	内燃机
Ministry of Industry and Information Technology (MIIT)	工业和信息化部（工信部）
come up with	提出，拿出
one after another	相继地

1. Along with the development of automobile industry, varied cars are produced for different consumers but customer buying criteria never change.

随着汽车产业的发展，多种多样的车被生产以满足不同的消费者需求，但客户的购买标准永远不会改变。

2. Electric vehicles (we call them "EVs" in this report) are propelled by an electric motor powered by rechargeable battery packs.

电动汽车（本文简称为"EVs"）由一个电动机驱动，该电动机由可充电电池组供电。

3. Ministry of Industry and Information Technology (MIIT) announced recently that China will input over 100 million to support the production of New Energy Vehicles in the coming 10 years.

工业和信息化部（MIIT）部最近宣布，中国将在未来10年投入100多万元，以支持新能源汽车的生产。

4. As EVs have several problems to be promoted, the China's government should unveil new policies especially for the high cost in order to enhance purchasing power from citizens.

针对电动车推广过程中面临的问题，中国政府应推出新的政策，特别是针对高成本方面，以提高公民的购买力。

Unit 3

A. Text

Building-Integrated Photovoltaic

Building-integrated photovoltaic (Figure 3-12) electric power systems not only produce electricity, they are also part of the building. For example, a BIPV skylight is an integral component of the building envelope as well as a solar electric energy system that generates electricity for the building. These solar systems are thus multifunctional construction materials.

Figure 3-12　Building-integrated photovoltaic electric power system

The standard element of a BIPV system is the PV module. Individual solar cells are interconnected and encapsulated on various materials to form a module. Modules are strung together in an electrical series with cables and wires to form a PV array. Direct or diffuse light (usually sunlight) shining on the solar cells induces the photovoltaic effect, generating unregulated DC electric power. This DC power can be used, stored in a battery system, or fed into an inverter that transforms and synchronizes the power into AC electricity. The electricity can be used in the building or exported to a utility company through a grid interconnection.

A wide variety of BIPV systems are available in today's markets. Most of them can be grouped into two main categories: facade systems and roofing systems. Facade systems include curtain wall products, spandrel panels, and glazing. Roofing systems include tiles, shingles, standing seam products, and skylights. This sourcebook illustrates how PV modules can be designed as aesthetically integrated building components (such as awnings) and as entire structures (such as bus shelters). BIPV is sometimes the optimal method of installing renewable energy systems in urban, built-up areas where undeveloped land is both scarce and expensive.

The fundamental first step in any BIPV application is to maximize energy efficiency within the building's energy demand or load. This way, the entire energy system can be optimized. Holistically designed BIPV systems will reduce a building's energy demand from the electric utility grid while generating electricity on site and performing as the weathering skin of the building. Roof and wall systems can provide R-value to diminish undesired thermal transference. Windows, skylights, and facade shelves can be designed to increase day lighting opportunities in interior spaces. PV awnings can be designed to reduce unwanted glare and heat gain. This integrated approach, which brings together energy conservation, energy efficiency, building envelope design, and PV technology and placement, maximizes energy savings and makes the most of opportunities to use BIPV systems.

New Words and Expressions

integral ['intigrəl]	adj.	完整的，整体的
multifunctional [ˌmʌlti'fʌŋkʃənl]	adj.	多功能的
individual [ˌindi'vidjuəl]	adj.	个别的，单独的
utility [ju:'tiləti]	n.	效用，有用
diminish [di'miniʃ]	v.	（使）减少，（使）变小
interior [in'tiəriə]	adj.	内部的，内的
awning ['ɔ:niŋ]	n.	遮阳篷，雨篷
noteworthy ['nəutˌwə:ði]	adj.	值得注目的，显著的
purchase ['pə:tʃəs]	vt.	买，购买

Technical Terms

building-integrated photovoltaic (BIPV)　　光伏建筑一体化
civic construction　　　　　　　　　　　　城市的建设

communicative area	通信领域
surface pressure	表面压力
impact strength	冲击强度
solar projects for new villages	太阳能建设新农村工程

Notes

1. Building-integrated photovoltaic (BIPV) electric power systems not only produce electricity, they are also part of the building. For example, a BIPV skylight is an integral component of the building envelope as well as a solar electric energy system that generates electricity for the building.

光伏建筑一体化（BIPV）电力系统不仅生产用电，它们也是建筑的一部分。例如，光伏建筑一体化天窗是建筑围护结构的一部分，同时又是太阳能发电系统的一个组成部分，用于建筑供电。

2. This sourcebook illustrates how PV modules can be designed as aesthetically integrated building components (such as awnings) and as entire structures (such as bus shelters).

资料将说明如何将光伏组件设计成美观集成建筑构件（如遮阳篷），或作为整个结构（如公共汽车候车亭）。

3. The fundamental first step in any BIPV application is to maximize energy efficiency within the building's energy demand or load.

任何BIPV应用中的第一步是在建筑物或负载的能源需求内，最大限度地提高能源利用效率。

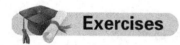

Exercises

1. Put the following phrases into English:
① 太阳能交通信号灯工程
② 小区风光互补系统
③ 光伏发电系统的应用
④ 光伏建筑一体化（BIPV）并网电站的应用与发展

2. Decide whether the following statements are true or false:
① The standard element of a BIPV system is the PV module.
② Holistically designed BIPV systems will reduce a building's energy demand from the electric utility grid while generating electricity on site and performing as the weathering skin of the building.
③ The U.S. government, with more than half a million facilities, is the largest energy consumer in the world.

3. **Translate the following sentences:**

① Building integrated photovoltaic system (BIPV), as the mean of utilizing solar energy, will make a significant contribution to the promotion of power industry in China and the development of ecological building. This paper analyzes and compares solar energy in main land and Hong Kong of China. The results show that the potential market of BIPV is very attractive.

② This paper describes the technology of BIPV, and the policies, programs and projects in US which promote the development of BIPV.

③ The advantages of Building Integrated Photovoltaic (BIPV) and the system structure are introduced in detail; the development trend of BIPV is also mentioned.

B. Reading

Power Station on Desert

BEIJING, Jan 10 (Xinhua)—Two large solar power plants will be built in the western plateau provinces of Qinghai and Yunnan in 2009, with the expectation for China to cut domestic reliance on coal and oil.

The Qinghai project, a gig watt-level solar station (Figure 3-13), will begin the first phase construction in 2009. The plant was funded by an initial investment of 1 billion Yuan (about 146 million U.S. dollars). It could become the world's largest when completed, according to a recent joint statement of the developers.

Figure 3-13 Power stations on desert

The NASDAQ-listed China Technology Development Group Corp. and the private-owned Qinghai New Energy Group are overseeing the design, construction, installation and operation of the station.

The government of Haixi Autonomous Prefecture of Mongolia and Tibet nationalities, where the project is located, signed an agreement with the two companies to help them acquire land, subsidies and project approvals from the central government.

Roughly a month ago, the southwestern Yunnan Province announced it would begin construction of a 166-megawatt solar plant with an investment of 9.1 billion Yuan—the largest in China at the time of the announcement.

Yang Minying, a researcher of the Chinese Academy of Social Sciences, said construction of the two projects would take time, but developing renewable energy resources is an irresistible trend in China.

Statistics from the China Renewable Energy Society showed more than two thirds of China's land receives more than 2,200 hours sunshine annually, more than many other regions of similar latitude such as Europe and Japan, which gives China a potential solar energy reserve equivalent to 1,700 billion tons of coal.

China is now the world's largest producer of solar heaters and the third largest manufacturer of photovoltaic cells, the National Development and Reform Commission (N.D.R.C.) statistics show.

However, N.D.R.C. pointed out, China still lags far behind other countries in solar power generation due to the high cost, limited government subsidies and market access.

The N.D.R.C. drafted a long-term plan for renewable energy use in 2007 and promised that the government would provide stimulus policies to encourage companies involved to develop renewable energy sources.

"The cost of solar generation is still relatively high compared with the developed solar markets—Germany and Japan," said Charles Yonts, a solar and clean-tech analyst with the HK-based brokerage CLSA.

"But, we will see costs come down rapidly as installers gain more experience," he added.

In a law passed in 2005 by the National People's Congress, China's top legislature, China set a goal to increase the share of renewable energy resources to 10 percent of China's total energy consumption by 2020.

"Effective development of renewable energy sources in China need careful investigation and a combination of different energy sources such as wind, solar and miasma," said Yang Minying.

China's first grid-connected solar power station in desert enters operation.

New Words and Expressions

plateau ['plætəu]	n.	高地，高原
gigawatt ['dʒigəwɔt]	n.	十亿瓦特
oversee [,əuvə'si:]	v.	俯瞰，监视，检查
acquire [ə'kwaiə]	vt.	获得，学到
roughly ['rʌfli]	adv.	概略地，粗糙地
renerable [ri'nju:əbl]	adj.	可更新的，可恢复的
latitude ['lætitju:d]	n.	纬度，范围

potential [pəu'tenʃəl]　　　　　adj. 潜在的，可能的
lag [læg]　　　　　　　　　　vt. 落后于
legislature ['ledʒisleitʃə]　　　　n. 立法机关，立法机构
miasma [mi'æzmə]　　　　　　n. 沼气

 Technical Terms

Chinese Academy of Social Sciences　　中国社会科学研究院
gigawatt-level solar station　　　　　　十亿瓦级太阳能电站
The National Development and Reform Commission (NDRC)　国家发展与改革委员会（NDRC）
The China Renewable Energy Society　国家可再生能源学会

 Notes

1. Two large solar power plants will be built in the western plateau provinces of Qinghai and Yunnan in 2009, with the expectation for China to cut domestic reliance on coal and oil.

2009年，将在西部高原省份青海、云南建立两个大型太阳能发电厂，与此同时，期望降低国内对煤炭和石油的依赖。

2. Roughly a month ago, the southwestern Yunnan Province announced it would begin construction of a 166-megawatt solar plant with an investment of 9.1 billion yuan—the largest in China at the time of the announcement.

大约一个月前，西南部的云南省宣布将投资91亿人民币开始建设一个166兆瓦的太阳能发电厂——迄今为止中国最大的光伏电站。

3. In a law passed in 2005 by the National People's Congress, China's top legislature, China set a goal to increase the share of renewable energy resources to 10 percent of China's total energy consumption by 2020.

中国在2005年通过一项法律，由全国人民代表大会（中国最高立法机关），设定了一个目标，增加可再生能源的份额，实现到2020年占中国能源消费总量的10％。

Part IV Wind Power

Unit 1

A. Text

Applications and Wind Industry

The main applications are the generation of electricity and water pumping. Except for the installed capacity for wind farms, the other numbers are best estimates, as data are difficult to acquire. Applications for generation of electricity are divided into the following categories: utility-scale wind farms; small wind turbines, which include remote and stand-alone systems; distributed; wind-diesel; village power (generally hybrid systems); and telecommunications (high-reliability hybrid systems). Many village power systems use photovoltaic panels with battery storage, 1 to 3 days. There are wind hybrid systems and some wind power systems for village power. In some cases village power has diesel/gas for the backup. Stand-alone systems generally have batteries for storage.

There are wind-assists, where two power sources work in parallel to produce power on demand, and stand-alone systems. All wind turbines connected to the utility grid are wind-assist systems. In terms of size, wind turbines range from the utility-scale megawatt turbines for wind farms to small systems ($\leqslant$100kW) also connected to the grid to the 20~300W remote units for sailboats and households, primarily in the developing world, some people refer to these as micro wind turbines. Be careful of some vendors claiming that micro wind turbines will produce electricity cheaper than utility-scale wind turbines, as all you need to do is to connect a large number of them together.

 New Words and Expressions

utility-scale [juːˈtilətiskeil]	adj. 可使用的，高功效的
turbine [ˈtəːbin]	n. 涡轮（机），叶轮（机）
remote [riˈməut]	adj. 遥远的，偏僻的，久远的
distributed [diˈstribjutid]	adj. 分布的
wind-diesel [waindˈdizl]	n. 风柴油
battery [ˈbætəri]	n. 电池
storage [ˈstɔridʒ]	n. 储存

wind-assist [ˌwaindəˈsist]	n. 风力协助
megawatt [ˈmegəˌwɑt]	n. 兆瓦
vendor [ˈvendə]	n. 供应商
telecommunication [ˌtelikəˌmjunəˈkeʃən]	n. 电信

water pumping	水泵
installed capacity	装机容量
wind farm	风电场
utility grid	电网

Notes

1. Except for the installed capacity for wind farms, the other numbers are best estimates, as data are difficult to acquire.

因为这些数据是很难获得的,所以除了风力发电厂的装机容量外,其他的数据最好是估算。

2. There are wind-assists, where two power sources work in parallel to produce power on demand, and stand-alone systems.

有风能辅助和独立两种系统,其中风能辅助系统中两种能源(太阳能和风能互补)一起工作产生需求的电力。

3. Be careful of some vendors claiming that micro wind turbines will produce electricity cheaper than utility-scale wind turbines, as all you need to do is to connect a large number of them together.

要小心一些厂商所声称的微型风力发电机比实用的风力涡轮机发电更便宜的说法,因为你需要将大量微型机连接在一起。

Exercises

1. Put the following phrases into English:
① 风电场   ② 装机容量   ③ 涡轮机   ④ 水泵
⑤ 风光互补   ⑥ 混合动力系统 ⑦ 电网   ⑧ 电池

2. Decide whether the following statements are true or false:

① There are wind hybrid systems and wind power systems for village power.

② The all numbers are best estimates, as data are difficult to acquire.

③ There are wind-assists, where two power sources work in parallel to produce power on demand, and stand-alone systems.

④ The micro wind turbines will produce electricity cheaper than utility-scale wind turbines.

B. Reading

Wind Industry, 2000~2010

Wind turbines are now a part of the planning process for new electric plants in many countries. Europe continues to lead in installed capacity, development of multi-megawatt turbines, and manufacturing. Global producers of equipment for electric power plants, general electric (Enron), United States, and Siemens (Bonus), Germany, became manufacturers by purchasing wind turbine companies. Vestas, which absorbed NEG-Micon, is still the leading manufacturer of large wind turbines. For large machines, the three-blade, full-span, variable-pitch, upwind machines now dominate the market.

The most economical size of wind turbines has not been determined, as the trend has been larger machines for the wind farm market. However, in many locations, especially islands and other remote locations in the world, the infrastructure is the limitation for installation of megawatt wind turbines, for example, cranes. The larger wind turbines are now being developed for offshore.

In the United States, with the production tax credit and the Renewable Portfolio Standard in Texas, there was a resurgence of wind farm installations. In 2006, Texas (Figure 4-1) surpassed California in installed capacity, and a number of other states have passed renewable Portfolio standards. Since no wind turbines from the DOE program became major players in the commercial market, by 2009 the research project was changed to assist manufacturers, through the program area of the Low Speed Wind Technology Project. The cost-shared research and development projects with industry included a 2.5 MW wind turbine, clipper wind power; a modular power electronics package that can be scaled from small to megawatt wind turbines; a 1.5 MW direct-drive generator, Northern Power Systems; a prototype multi-megawatt low-wind-speed turbine, General Electric; and others.

Another emerging market is village electrification in developing countries. It is cheaper to have village power than to extend transmission lines. The primary source of energy will be renewable energy: solar, wind, hydro, and biomass. Many of these will be hybrid systems with batteries and diesel for firm power. Large lending institutions, such as the World Bank and national government aid programs, now realize there is an alternative to large-scale projects for producing power. Also, there are more manufacturers of small wind turbines, and manufacturers in the United States and China expanded their production.

Landowners now harvest the wind much as they harvest the sun for food and fiber. Since financing for large wind power plants requires millions of dollars, the landowner usually leases the land and receives a royalty form the energy produced by the wind turbines, similar to the oil and gas industry. The difference is that the wind resource can be

Part IV   Wind Power   61

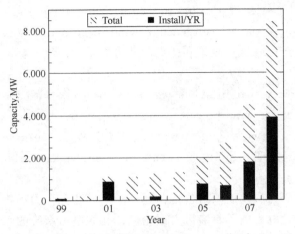

Figure 4-1 Wind farm capacity in Texas, number installed/year and cumulative. Capacity installed in 2008 was estimated at 3,900MW

fully determined before large amounts of money are invested, and even more important, the resource will not run out.

New Words and Expressions

upwind ['ʌp'wind]	adj./adv.	迎风的，逆风的
infrastructure ['infrə'strʌktʃə]	n.	公共建设，基础建设
crane [krein]	n.	起重机，吊车
offshore ['ɔ:fʃɔ:]	adj.	近岸的，近海的，离岸的，向海的
resurgence [ri'sə:dʒəns]	n.	复活，复苏，再现
hydro ['haidrəu]	n.	水
fiber ['faibə]	n.	纤维，纤维物质，纤维质料

Technical Terms

electric plant	发电厂
modular power electronics package	模块化的电力电子封装
village electrification	电气化村

Notes

1. However, in many locations, especially islands and other remote locations in the world, the infrastructure is the limitation for installation of megawatt wind turbines, for example, cranes.

然而，在许多地方，尤其是岛屿和其他偏远地区，基础设施，例如起重机，限制了大型风力涡轮机的安装。

2. In the United States, with the production tax credit and the Renewable Portfolio Standard in Texas, there was a resurgence of wind farm installations.

在美国,因为生产税收抵免政策和得克萨斯可再生能源组合标准,风力发电装备有复苏的迹象。

3. The cost-shared research and development projects with industry included a 2.5 MW wind turbine, clipper wind power; a modular power electronics package that can be scaled from small to megawatt wind turbines; a 1.5 MW direct-drive generator, Northern Power Systems; a prototype multi-megawatt low-wind-speed turbine, General Electric; and others.

商业成本分担的研究和发展项目包括:远程的2.5兆瓦风力涡轮机;可以按比例从小到兆瓦级划分的模块化电力电子封装风力涡轮机;北方电力系统的1.5兆瓦直接驱动发电机;通用电气的原型多兆瓦低风速涡轮机;等等。

4. The primary source of energy will be renewable energy: solar, wind, hydro, and biomass.

主要的能源来源将是可再生能源:太阳能、风能、水能和生物质能。

5. Also, there are more manufacturers of small wind turbines, and manufacturers in the United States and China expanded their production.

此外,小型风力涡轮机制造商更多一些,并且在美国和中国,这些制造商已在扩大生产。

6. The difference is that the wind resource can be fully determined before large amounts of money are invested, and even more important, the resource will not run out.

不同的是,风资源在大量的资金投入前可以完全被确定,而且更重要的是,风资源将不会被用完。

Unit 2

A. Text

Description of the System

The total system consists of the wind turbine and load. A typical wind turbine consists of the rotor (blades and hub), speed increaser (gearbox), conversion system, controls, and tower (Figure 4-2). The nacelle is the covering or enclosure. The output of the rotor, rotational kinetic energy, can be converted to electrical, mechanical, or thermal energy. Generally, it is electrical energy, so the conversion system is a generator.

Blade configuration may include a nonuniform platform (blade width and length), twist along the blade and variable (blades can be rotated) or fixed pitch. The pitch is the angle of the chord at the tip of the blade to the plane of rotation. The chord is the line from the nose to the tail of the airfoil.

Components for a large unit mounted on a bedplate are shown in Figure 4-3. Most large wind turbines, which are pitch regulated, have full-span (blade) control, and in this

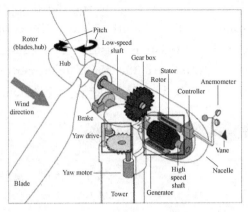

Figure 4-2 Schematic of major components for large wind turbine

Figure 4-3 Photos of components, Suzlon, 64m diameter, 1000kW, induction generator 4/6pole. Bottom right: Cutaway of gearbox, Winergy

case, electric motors are used to rotate, change the pitch of the blades. All blades must have the same pitch for all operational conditions.

For units connected to the utility grid, 50 or 60 Hz, the generators can be synchronous or induction connected directly to the grid through an inverter. Most direct current (DC) generators and permanent magnet alternators on small wind turbines do not have a speed increaser. One type of large wind turbine has no gearbox, which means it has very large generators. Some HAWTs use slip rings to transfer power and control signals from the top of the tower to ground level, while others have wire cords that have extra length for absorbing twist. After so much twist, it must be removed by yawing the turbine or by a manual disconnect. For large wind turbines, the transformer or a winch may be located in the nacelle. A total system is called a wind energy conversion system (WECS).

New Words and Expressions

rotor ['rəutə]	n.	转子，转片，旋转轮
blade [bleid]	n.	叶片，叶片状物，桨叶
hub [hʌb]	n.	(轮) 毂，(推进器的) 旋翼叶毂
gearbox ['giəbɔks]	n.	(汽车等的) 齿轮箱
nacelle [nə'sel]	n.	(飞机、飞船等的) 引擎舱，吊舱
rotational [rəu'teiʃənl]	adj.	旋转的，轮流的，循环的
nonuniform [nɔn'ju:nifɔ:m]	adj.	不均匀的
airfoil ['eəfɔil]	n.	机翼，螺旋桨
synchronous ['siŋkrənəs]	adj.	同周期的，同步
winch [wintʃ]	n.	绞盘，绞车，曲柄，摇柄

Technical Terms

speed increaser　　　　　　　　　增速器
permanent magnet alternator　　　永磁交流发电机

Notes

1. A typical wind turbine consists of the rotor (blades and hub), speed increaser (gearbox), conversion system, controls, and tower. The nacelle is the covering or enclosure.

一个典型的风力发电机由转子（叶片和轮毂）、增速器（变速箱）、转换系统、控制器和塔组成。发动机舱是盖子或外壳。

2. For units connected to the utility grid, 50 or 60 Hz, the generators can be synchronous or induction connected directly to the grid through an inverter.

用于要连接到 50 或 60 赫兹的公用电网，发电机可以通过一个逆变器同步或异步直接连接到网格。

3. One type of large wind turbine has no gearbox, which means it has very large generators.

有一种大型风力机没有变速箱，这意味着它有非常大的发电机。

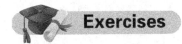

1. Put the following phrases into English:
① 风电场　　　② 装机容量　　　③ 涡轮机　　　④ 水泵
⑤ 风光互补　　⑥ 混合动力系统　⑦ 电网　　　　⑧ 电池

2. Decide whether the following statements are true or false:

① There are wind hybrid systems and some wind power systems for village power.

② The all numbers are best estimates, as data are difficult to acquire.

③ There are wind-assists, where two power sources work in parallel to produce power on demand, and stand-alone systems.

④ The micro wind turbines will produce electricity cheaper than utility-scale wind turbines.

B. Reading

Small Wind Turbines

Generally small horizontal-axis wind turbines are kept facing into the wind by a tail. The control mechanism to reduce power in high winds is that the rotor axis is offset from the pivot point, axis of connection to the tower (Figure 4-4). Therefore, there is more force on one side of the rotor than the other, which tries to move the rotor parallel to the wind; however, the wind force on the tail keeps the rotor perpendicular to the wind. For high winds the unequal force on the rotor is greater than the force of the tail; therefore, the rotor moves parallel to the wind. For very small rotors the tail may be fixed, and during medium to high winds with rapid change in direction, sometimes these wind turbines will turn completely around the yaw axis, a 360° revolution. Most of the wind turbines have a hinge for the tail, and for high winds, the rotor moves to a position closer to parallel to the tail, called furling. Then when the winds decrease, the tail returns to a position perpendicular to the rotor by a force due to springs or gravity. Dampers, like shock absorbers, can keep this movement from happening too rapidly, both for furling and for restoration to normal operation. The farm windmill uses springs, the length of which is adjustable for the restoring force. One mechanism to use gravity is to have the tail hinge at a slight inclined angle to the vertical plane.

Performance was measured for a 2kW wind turbine for water pumping for changes in the parameters of offset of the rotor axis to the yaw axis, length of tail boom, area of tail, and pitch angle. Four different tails and two different yaw axis offsets were tested because the furling behavior was critical to the performance. Overall, nine different configurations were tested, which included two sets of blades with different pitch angles to try to improve the performance at low wind speeds.

The pivot point does not have to be around the vertical axis (yaw); it can also be

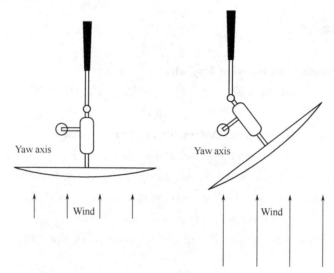

Figure 4-4　Diagram of rotor axis offset from yaw axis
with hinged tail for furling

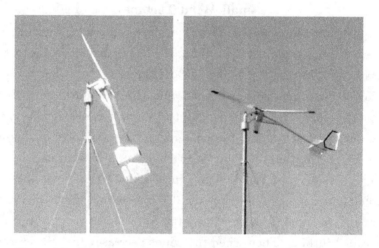

Figure 4-5　Rotor axis offset from horizontal pivot point for control

about a horizontal axis, which would produce vertical furling. The rotor and generator on the North Wind high-reliability turbine had a horizontal pivot for the rotor and generator, a coil spring damper, and the restoring mechanism was gravity. Another horizontal pivot was unique in that the rotor was downwind and the tail with flat plate and fins hung down (moderate winds to 13m/s). In high winds the force of the wind on the rotor and also on the flat part of the tail moved the tail and rotor, alternator to the horizontal position, and vertical furling (Figure 4-5). There is no hinge on the tail and the restoring force is gravity.

Small wind turbines are mostly mounted on pole and lattice towers. Very small wind turbines are mounted on almost anything, even on buildings, and of course on sailboats they are mounted on a short pole. A short pole is sometimes referred to as a stub mast.

New Words and Expressions

perpendicular [ˌpə:pən'dikjulə]   adj. 垂直的
hinge [hindʒ]   n. 铰链
damper ['dæmpə]   n. 阻尼器
spring [spriŋ]   n. 弹簧
adjustable [ə'dʒʌstəbl]   adj. 可调的
pivot ['pivət]   n. 枢轴

Technical Terms

yaw axis   偏航轴
shock absorber   减震器
pivot point   枢轴点

Notes

1. Generally small horizontal-axis wind turbines are kept facing into the wind by a tail. The control mechanism to reduce power in high winds is that the rotor axis is offset from the pivot point, axis of connection to the tower.

小型水平轴风力涡轮机通常都面对入风，为了减小强风的力度，控制机制就是转子轴偏移与它相连的枢轴点。

2. The pivot point does not have to be around the vertical axis (yaw); it can also be about a horizontal axis, which would produce vertical furling.

枢轴点不一定需要围绕垂直轴（偏航）；它也可以是一个水平轴，这样可以垂直弯曲。

3. The rotor and generator on the North Wind high-reliability turbine had a horizontal pivot for the rotor and generator, a coil spring damper, and the restoring mechanism was gravity.

North Wind 高可靠性风涡轮上的转子和发电机有一个水平枢纽和线圈弹簧阻尼器，靠重力恢复原位。

4. Small wind turbines are mostly mounted on pole and lattice towers. Very small wind turbines are mounted on almost anything, even on buildings, and of course on sailboats they are mounted on a short pole. A short pole is sometimes referred to as a stub mast.

小型风力涡轮机大多安装在杆子和塔上。非常小的风力涡轮机几乎可以安装在任何地方，甚至在建筑物上。当然，在帆船上它们都被安装在一根短柱上，短杆有时称为短桅杆。

Unit 3

A. Text

Power Electronic Solutions in Wind Farms

Today, and in the future, wind turbines will be sited in large concentrations with hundreds of megawatts of power capacity. Wind farms of this size will often be connected directly to the transmission grid and will, sooner or later, replace conventional power plants. This means that the wind turbines will be required to have power plant characteristics, namely, to be able to behave as active controllable components in the power system. Such large wind farms will be expected to meet very high technical demands, such as to perform frequency and voltage control, to regulate active and reactive power and to provide quick responses during transient and dynamic situations in the power system. The traditional wind turbines, where the active power is controlled by a simple pitching of the blades or by using a dumping device or by disconnecting the wind turbines, do not have such control capabilities and cannot contribute to power system stability as will be required. Storage technologies may be an option, too, but at the present such technologies are rather expensive. Also, they are not a satisfactory solution in the case of large wind farms, because of voltage stability issues. Power electronic technology will therefore become more and more attractive for large wind farms that will have to fulfill future high demands.

Presently, there are significant research activities to develop the electrical control layout of such wind farms with different types of power electronic converters in order for them to be able to comply with the high requirements and to be as cheap as possible to install. Many control topologies are being investigated and some are already being implemented in practice.

Depending on how the power electronic devices are used inside a wind farm, there are several different topology options, each with its particular advantages and disadvantages. The topology can include the following.

• A completely decentralized control structure with an internal AC network connected to the main grid, with each turbine in the wind farm having its own frequency converter and its own control system, has the advantage that each wind turbine can operate at its optimum level with respect to its local wind condition.

• A partly centralized, partly decentralized control structure where the power converter is 'split up' and the output of each turbine is locally rectified and fed into a DC network with the whole farm still connected through a central inverter, has been proposed by Dahlgren *et al*. (2000), who suggest making use of a multipole high voltage synchronous generator with permanent magnets. However, this solution has not yet been implemented in practice.

• A completely centralized control structure has a central power electronic converter connected at the wind farm's connection point. The turbines either could have SCIGs or could have WRSGs. The advantage of such structure is that the internal behavior of the wind turbines is separated from the grid behavior, and thus the wind farm is robust to possible failures of the grid. The disadvantage of this concept is that all wind turbines are rotating with the same average angular speed and not at an individual optimal speed, thereby giving up some of the features of the variable-speed concept, for each individual wind turbine.

An option of this concept is the centralized reactive power compensation topology with an advanced static VAR compensation (ASVC) unit. Reactive power compensation units are widely used in power systems in order to provide the reactive power balance and to improve voltage stability. ASVCs are inverters based on self-commutated switches (i.e. with full, continuous control of the reactive power). They have the advantage that, in the case of a voltage decrease (e.g. during a grid fault) their available maximum reactive power decreases more slowly compared with the static VAR compensation (SVC) units.

Another option is the use of a high-voltage DC (HVDC) link as power transmission. Such an installation is running on Gotland, Sweden. All wind turbines are connected to the same power converter, and the entire wind farm is connected to the public supply grid through another power converter. These two converters are connected to each other through a long, HVDC link cable.

The application of power electronic technology in large wind farms seems thus to be very promising. It plays a key role in complying with the high requirements that utility companies impose on wind farms. This technology therefore needs substantial additional research and development.

New Words and Expressions

conventional [kən'venʃənl]   adj. 正常的，传统的
topology [təu'pɔlədʒi]   n. 拓扑
decentralized [di:'sentrəlaizd]   adj. 分散的
centralized ['səntrəlaizd]   adj. 集中的

Technical Terms

power capacity   功率容量
power plant   发电厂

permanent magnet 永久磁铁
advanced static VAR compensation（ASVC） 先进的静态无功补偿

Notes

1. Wind farms of this size will often be connected directly to the transmission grid and will, sooner or later, replace conventional power plants.

这种规模的风力发电场往往会被直接连接到输电网，迟早会取代传统的发电厂。

2. Such large wind farms will be expected to meet very high technical demands，such as to perform frequency and voltage control, to regulate active and reactive power and to provide quick responses during transient and dynamic situations in the power system.

这样的大型风电场将有望达到非常高的技术要求，如执行频率和电压控制、有功无功调节和期间提供的电力系统暂态和动态情况的快速反应。

3. A completely decentralized control structure with an internal AC network connected to the main grid, with each turbine in the wind farm having its own frequency converter and its own control system, has the advantage that each wind turbine can operate at its optimum level with respect to its local wind condition.

一个完全分散、内部由交流网络连接到主网格的控制结构，其每个涡轮机在风电场有它自己的频率转换器和控制系统，每个风力机可以就其当地的风力条件工作在其最佳水平，这是它的优势。

4. A completely centralized control structure has a central power electronic converter connected at the wind farm's connection point.

一个完全的集中控制结构有一个中央电力电子转换器连接在风电场的连接点。

5. It plays a key role in complying with the high requirements that utility companies impose on wind farms. This technology therefore needs substantial additional research and development.

它在满足公共事业公司对风电场高要求上发挥了关键作用。这种技术仍需要大量的额外的研究与发展。

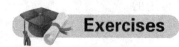

1. Put the following phrases into English：
① 功率容量　② 发电厂　③ 拓扑结构
④ 无功补偿　⑤ 永久磁铁　⑥ 兆瓦

2. Decide whether the following statements are true or false：
① Wind farms of this size will often be connected directly to the transmission grid and will, sooner or later, replace conventional power plants.

② A completely decentralized control structure with an internal DC network connected to the main grid, with each turbine in the wind farm having its own frequency converter and its own control system, has the advantage that each wind turbine can operate at its optimum level with respect to its local wind condition.

③ A completely centralized control structure has a central power electronic converter connected at the wind farm's connection point.

④ The application of power electronic technology in small wind farms seems thus to be very promising.

B. Reading

Design of Wind Turbines

The design of wind turbines has developed from a background of work on propellers, airplanes, and helicopters. Computer codes developed for analyzing aerodynamics, forces, and vibration have been modified for wind turbines. Theory and experimental procedures are well developed, and no scientific breakthroughs are needed for wind turbines. However, there are problems of predicting loads from unsteady aerodynamics. These loads lead to fatigue and less life than predicted by the design codes. Part of the time, wind turbine blades operate in regions of large attack angles, which is quite different than for airplane wings.

Someone made the comment that you could use brooms for blades and the rotor would turn. Of course, the efficiency would be low, control would be a problem, and the strength would not be adequate. A large number of airfoils were developed for wings on planes and sailplanes, which were later used for wind turbine blades.

In the beginning the aerospace industry thought that the design of wind turbines and their construction would simply be the transfer of technical knowledge from airplanes and helicopters. However, this was an erroneous conclusion. One big difference is that airplanes and helicopters move in response to large loads from wind gusts, whereas a wind turbine is tied to the ground. Because power in the wind increases as the cube of the wind speed, the blades must have the strength and flexibility to withstand the high variable loads, and then there must be a control mechanism for shedding power in high winds.

There has been a lot of research and development, primarily by national labs and universities, and later by the manufacturers of wind turbines, which has resulted in today's wind industry. The design of wind turbines requires a broad cross section of knowledge: aerodynamics, mechanical engineering, electrical engineering, electronics, materials and industrial engineering, civil engineering, and meteorology. The design process is iterative from first concept to the final design. Remember, it is easier to fix problems at the design stage than to have the cost of retrofits in the field.

New Words and Expressions

propeller [prəˈpelə]	n. 螺旋桨，推进器
helicopter [ˈhelikɔptə]	n. 直升机
vibration [vaiˈbreiʃən]	n. 感受，共鸣，振荡，颤动
modify [ˈmɔdifai]	v. 缓和，减轻，更改
aerodynamics [ˌɛərəudaiˈnæmiks]	n. 空气动力学，航空动力学
broom [bru:m]	n. 扫帚，长柄刷
airfoil [ˈɛəfɔil]	n. 机翼，螺旋桨
erroneous [iˈrəuniəs]	adj. 错误的，不正确的
meteorology [ˌmi:tjəˈrɔlədʒi]	n. 气象学，气象状态
iterative [ˈitərətiv]	adj. 反复的
retrofit [ˈretrəfit]	n. 式样翻新

Technical Terms

experimental procedure	实验程序
shedding power	流电源
wind industry	风电产业

Notes

1. Part of the time, wind turbine blades operate in regions of large attack angles, which is quite different than for airplane wings.

有些时候，风力机叶片在大迎角的区域工作，这是和飞机的翅膀有很大区别的。

2. A large number of airfoils were developed for wings on planes and sailplanes, which were later used for wind turbine blades.

大量用在飞机和滑翔机上的机翼，后来被用于风力涡轮机叶片。

3. One big difference is that airplanes and helicopters move in response to large loads from wind gusts, whereas a wind turbine is tied to the ground.

一个很大的不同是：飞机和直升机针对大负荷强风移动，而风力机是绑在地上的。

4. There has been a lot of research and development, primarily by national labs and universities, and later by the manufacturers of wind turbines, which has resulted in today's wind industry.

现有的很多研究和发展，先是由国家实验室和大学，后来是由风力涡轮机制造商实现，这样就有了今天的风电产业。

Unit 4

A. Text

Water Pumping

The pumping of water and sailboats are the oldest and longest-term uses of wind power. The two common examples of mechanical water pumping are the historical Dutch windmill for pumping large volumes of water from a low lift and the farm windmill for pumping small volumes of water from a high lift.

For mechanical windmills or wind turbines the important considerations are the power in the wind and how that power can be transferred by the system. This means that the characteristics of the wind turbine (primarily the rotor) and the characteristics of the pump are combined in an operating system. The type of pump in many cases dictates the mode of operation of the rotor and how the rotational shaft power is transferred to pump power. Of course, the size of the system depends on the dynamic pumping head and the quantity of water to be pumped. For the farm windmill, the efficiency depends on the load matching of the rotor to a positive displacement type, in general a reciprocating pump (piston).

The American farm windmill is still in widespread use around the world for pumping low volumes of water from wells or boreholes. It is estimated that there are around 80,000 operating in the Southern High Plains of the United States. World production is estimated at 3,000 per year. The American farm windmill is well designed for pumping small volumes of water for livestock and residences, and the design has not changed since the 1920s and 1930s. The only change has been in materials used for bearings and the use of plastic pumps and drop pipes.

The American farm windmill is characterized by a high-solidity rotor (also called a wheel) consisting of fifteen to eighteen blades (also called vanes), which are normally made in a slight curve (Figure 4-6). The large number of blades provides a high starting torque that is needed for operating the piston pump. Most units have back gearing (reduction in speed) that transfers the rotating motion of the rotor to a reciprocating motion for pumping water. All wind turbines have a way to reduce efficiency and not capture all the energy possible at high winds. On the farm wind windmill the rotor axis and yaw axis are offset to rotate (yaw) the rotor out of the wind. This is called furling. At low wind speeds, the tail and the spring bring the rotor perpendicular to the wind.

The rotor has a peak power coefficient (C_p) of about 30% at a tip speed ratio of around 0.8. The efficiency for a reciprocating displacement pump is essentially constant at 80% over the operating range of wind speeds. The overall annual efficiency (wind to water pumped) is around 5% to 6%.

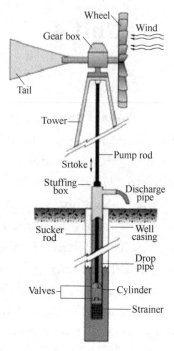

Figure 4-6 Schematic diagram of the American farm windmill

In the 1970s and 1980s, different research groups and manufacturers attempted to improve the performance of the farm windmill and reduce the const. many of these projects were designed to pump water in developing countries. Designers believed that the performance could be increased by the following changes:

① Reduce the solidity (reduce the number of blades or area of blades), which means higher rotor rpm.

② Change the characteristics of the pump by using variable stroke or variable volume to match the characteristics of the rotor.

③ Develop a windmill of the low wind regions of the tropics.

④ Counterbalance the weight of the rods, pump, and water column.

The Agricultural research Service, USCA, and the alternative Energy Institute, WTAMU, have tested some of these concepts in their cooperative program on wind energy for rural applications. A company in South Africa has a windmill with a rotating helix pump.

Costs can be reduced by using local materials, local light industry manufacturers, and new windmills designed for developing countries. One option is the use of the Savonius rotor for low volume, shallow water. Another option is a wind turbine driving an air compressor and an airlift pump. However, the problem is still the same: the rotor is connected to a constant-torque device.

New Words and Expressions

windmill ['windmil]	n.	风车
reciprocate [ri'siprəkeit]	v.	往复运动
piston ['pistən]	n.	活塞
well [wel]	n.	井
borehole ['bɔːhəul]	n.	钻孔
livestock ['laivstɔk]	n.	牲畜
residence ['rezidəns]	n.	居民
vane [vein]	n.	叶片
curve [kəːv]	n.	弯，弧线
perpendicular [,pəːpən'dikjulə]	adj.	垂直的
volume ['vɔljum]	n.	体积
counterbalance [,kauntə'bæləns]	v.	平衡
stroke [strəuk]	n.	行程，冲程

Technical Terms

drop pipe	水管
rotational shaft power	旋转轴功率
starting torque	启动转矩
power coefficient	功率系数
helix pump	螺旋泵

Notes

1. The two common examples of mechanical water pumping are the historical Dutch windmill for pumping large volumes of water from a low lift and the farm windmill for pumping small volumes of water from a high lift.

两个常见的机械抽水泵的例子：一个是历史上的荷兰风车，它从低水位抽出大量的水；另一个是从高处抽出较小体积水的农场风车。

2. For the farm windmill, the efficiency depends on the load matching of the rotor to a positive displacement type, in general a reciprocating pump (piston).

对于农场风车，效率取决于风车转子和一个正排量式的一般为往复水泵的负载匹配情况。

3. Costs can be reduced by using local materials, local light industry manufacturers, and new windmills designed for developing countries.

可以通过使用当地材料、轻工制造商和为发展中国家设计的新风车来降低成本。

4. Another option is a wind turbine driving an air compressor and an airlift pump.

However, the problem is still the same: the rotor is connected to a constant-torque device.

另一种选择是一个风力涡轮机驱动空气压缩机和空运泵。然而，问题仍然是相同的：转子连接到一个恒定扭矩的设备。

Exercises

1. Put the following phrases into English:
① 活塞　　　② 平衡　　　③ 风车　　　④ 水管
⑤ 启动转矩　⑥ 螺旋桨　　⑦ 传动装置　⑧ 功率因素

2. Decide whether the following statements are true or false:

① For the farm windmill, the efficiency depends on the load matching of the rotor to a positive displacement type, in general a reciprocating pump.

② The American farm windmill is still in widespread use around the world for pumping low volumes of water from wells or boreholes.

③ Most units have front gearing that transfers the rotating motion of the rotor to a reciprocating motion for pumping water.

④ Costs can be reduced by using local materials, local light industry manufacturers, and new windmills designed for developed countries.

B. Reading

Wind Chargers

As electricity became practical, isolated locations were too far from generating plants and transmission lines were too costly. Therefore, a number of manufacturers built stand-alone wind systems for generating electricity (Figure 4-7 and Figure 4-8), based on a

Figure 4-7　Windcharger, 100W, direct current, with flap air brakes. At USDA-ARS wind test station, Bushland, Texas

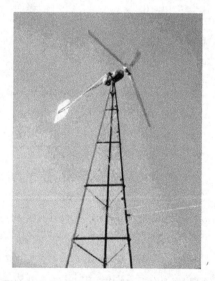

Figure 4-8　Jacobs, 4kW, direct current generator. It was still in use in the 1970s on a farm near Vega, Texas

propeller type rotor with two or three blades. Most of the wind chargers had a direct current generator, 6 to 32 volts (V), and some of the later models were 110V. The electricity was stored in batteries, and these wet-cell, lead-acid batteries required careful maintenance for long life.

These systems with two or three propeller blades are quite different from the farm windmill, which had a large number of blades covering most of the rotor swept area. The farm windmill is well engineered for pumping low volumes of water; however, it is too inefficient for generating electricity because the blade design and large number of blades means slow rotational speed of the rotor.

The wind chargers became obsolete in the United States when inexpensive electricity (subsidized) became available from rural electric cooperatives in the 1940s and 1950s. After the energy crisis of 1973, a number of these units were repaired for personal use or to sell. Small companies also imported wind machines from Australia and Europe to sell in the United States during the 1970s.

New Words and Expressions

battery ['bætəri]	n. 电池；蓄电池
maintenance ['meintinəns]	n. 维持，维修，保养
subsidize ['sʌbsidaiz]	v. 给……津贴，补助
import [im'pɔːt]	v. 进口，输入

Technical Terms

generating plant	发电厂
farm windmill	农场风车
rural electric cooperative	农村电力合作社

Notes

1. As electricity became practical, isolated locations were too far from generating plants and transmission lines were too costly. Therefore, a number of manufacturers built stand-alone wind systems for generating electricity, based on a propeller type rotor with two or three blades.

随着用电变得越来越实用，而孤立的地方离发电厂太远，传输线太过昂贵。因此，一些厂家建立独立的风力发电系统，其基于一个带两个或者三个叶片的螺旋桨型转子。

2. These systems with two or three propeller blades are quite different from the farm windmill, which had a large number of blades covering most of the rotor swept area.

这些两个或三个螺旋桨叶片的系统和农场风车有很大的不同，农场风车上有许多叶片，它们覆盖了大多数转子扫过的面积。

3. The wind chargers became obsolete in the United States when inexpensive electricity (subsidized) became available from rural electric cooperatives in the 1940s and 1950s. After the energy crisis of 1973, a number of these units were repaired for personal use or to sell.

在20世纪40~50年代，美国可以从农村电力合作社很方便地得到廉价电力（补贴），那时风力充电器成为过时。1973年能源危机以后，许多风力充电器被修复以用作个人使用或者出售。

Part V Other New Energy

Unit 1

A. Text

First Nuclear Power Plants

The United States (U. S.) gained a head start on nuclear technology because of work on the nuclear weapons' program. The U. S. Atomic Energy Commission (AEC) took the lead in the research and development of a controlled chain reaction applicable to energy generation. Many hypotheses were put forward and several promising paths were explored. But real momentum developed when U. S. Navy Captain Hyman G. Richover established a division of the AEC in order to develop a nuclear power plant for a submarine. This program, established in 1949, was to be the forerunner of commercial generating stations in the U. S. and worldwide. Rickover's concept bore fruit in 1953. The technology and materials development pioneered by his team became the foundation of future U. S. nuclear plants. The AEC concurrently established a large testing site at Arco, Idaho, where in 1951, a fast neutron reactor produced the first electricity (100kW) generated from controlled fission.

The world's first civil nuclear power station became operational in mid 1954 at Obninsk in the former Soviet Union, with a generating capacity of 5 MW. This was approximately the same level of energy output as in the U. S. submarine design.

On December 2, 1957, the Shippingport reactor in Pennsylvania began operations with a power output of 60MW. This event heralded the beginning for the generation of commercial power plants in the U. S.

Several basic concepts were explored, developed and demonstrated throughout the world during this period. The U. S. submarine and Shippingport plants were pressurized water reactors (PWR) utilizing subcooled water as the fuel coolant. Water also served as the moderator. The soviets developed enriched uranium, graphite-moderated, water-cooled designs. The British and French engineers explored natural uranium, graphite-moderated, carbon dioxide cooled station. In all of these designs the coolant (gas, liquid metal or pressurized water) transferred heat to a heat exchanger, where secondary water was vaporized to provide steam, which in turn drove the turbine-generator. The other major competing approach in the U. S. was the boiling water reactor (BWR). This was similar to the PWR except that the need for a heat exchanger to transfer heat from the coolant to the secondary steam cycle was eliminated by boiling water in the reactor core and this radioactive steam can be used to drive the turbine.

Two main types of reactor fuel evolved—enriched and natural uranium, in the early stages of nuclear power development only the two major nuclear powers. The U.S. and the Soviet Union had sufficient fuel production capacity for civilian power production using enriched uranium. Therefore, natural uranium was chosen as the principal fuel in the United Kingdom (U.K.), France, Canada and Sweden. While the enriched uranium-fueled plants were smaller, thus requiring a lower initial investment, over the life of the plant the higher cost of the enriched fuel meant that economically these plants were on a par with those using natural uranium. As these six countries had launched programs to build civil, commercial nuclear power stations, many other countries were involved in collaboration in order to have access to this technology.

New Words and Expressions

hypothesis [hai'pɔθisis]	n.	假设
promising ['prɔmisiŋ]	adj.	有希望的，有前途的
momentum [məu'mentəm]	n.	势头，动量
forerunner ['fɔːrʌnə]	n.	先驱者，前兆
concurrent [kən'kʌrənt]	adj.	同时发生的，共有的
operational [ɔpə'reiʃənəl]	adj.	操作上的，用于操作的
mid [mid]	adj.	中部的，当中的
herald ['herəld]	v.	宣布，预示……的来临
pressurize ['preʃəraiz]	v.	对……加压，使加压
utilize ['juːtilaiz]	v.	利用
graphite ['græfait]	n.	石墨
moderate ['mɔdərit]	v.	使缓和，节制
civilian [si'viljən]	adj.	民用的，民间的
par [pɑː]	n.	平价，制定等价
collaboration [kəlæbə'reiʃən]	n.	合作，协作
atomic [ə'tɔmik]	adj.	原子的，原子能的
subcool [sʌb'kuːl]	v.	使过冷，使过度冷却
enrich [in'ritʃ]	v.	使丰富，浓缩
vaporize ['veipəraiz]	v.	（使）蒸发，（使）汽化
radioactive [ˌreidiəu'æktiv]	adj.	放射性的，放射引起的

Technical Terms

generating capacity	发电容量，发电能力

pressurized water reactor (PWR)　　　加压水（冷却）反应堆
subcooled water　　　　　　　　　　低温冷却水
enriched uranium　　　　　　　　　　浓缩铀
boiling water reactor (BWR)　　　　　沸水反应堆
heat exchanger　　　　　　　　　　　热交换器
reactor core　　　　　　　　　　　　反应堆堆芯
radioactive steam　　　　　　　　　　放射性蒸汽

Notes

1. the U. S. Atomic Energy Commission (AEC) 美国原子能委员会
2. commercial generating station 商用发电站
3. Idaho 爱达荷（美国州名）
4. a fast neutron reactor 快速中子反应堆
5. kW [＝kilowatt] 千瓦（特）
6. the Soviet Union 苏联
7. MW [＝megawatt] 兆瓦
8. Shippingport 希坪港（美国地名）
9. Pennsylvania 宾夕法尼亚（美国州名）
10. commercial power plant 商用动力（电）厂
11. on a par with （和……）同等（或同价）
12. the United Kingdom (U. K.) 联合王国，指英国
13. The world's first civil nuclear power station became operational in mid 1954 at Obninsk in the former Soviet Union, with a generating capacity of 5 MW. This was approximately the same level of energy output as in the U. S. submarine design.

世界上第一个民用核电站于1954年在苏联的奥布宁斯克开始运作，其具有发电能力5兆瓦。这和美国潜艇设计的能源输出具有几乎相同的水平。

14. The U. S. and the Soviet Union had sufficient fuel production capacity for civilian power production using enriched uranium. Therefore, natural uranium was chosen as the principal fuel in the United Kingdom (U. K.), France, Canada and Sweden.

美国和苏联有足够的燃料的生产能力来使用浓缩铀生产民用电力。天然铀在英国、法国、加拿大和瑞典被选为主要燃料。

Exercises

1. Put the following phrases into English：
① 热交换器　　② 核反应堆　　③ 浓缩铀　　④ 低温冷却水

⑤ 千瓦　　　⑥ 沸水反应堆　　⑦ 商用发电站　　⑧ 快速中子反应堆

2. Decide whether the following statements are true or false:

① Natural uranium was chosen as the principal fuel in the U. S., the Soviet Union, the United Kingdom (U. K.), France, Canada and Sweden.

② The world's first civil nuclear power station became operational in mid 1954 at Obninsk in the former Soviet Union, with a generating capacity of 5 MW. This was the much less level of energy output than in the U. S. submarine design.

③ On December 2, 1957, the Shippingport reactor in Pennsylvania began operations with a power output of 60MW. This event heralded the beginning for the generation of commercial power plants in the U. S.

④ Two main types of reactor fuel evolved —enriched and natural uranium, in the early stages of nuclear power development only the two major nuclear powers.

B. Reading

Safety

Although the safety of a nuclear power plant is directly linked to the decision taken at the design stage and to the care taken in pre-construction studies and construction itself, it is only really in operation that nuclear safety can be seen in all its various facets, i. e. the risk of accident due to weaknesses in the design, insufficient quality or operational error.

1. Maintaining the Safety Level

In order to maintain the level of safety, it is first of all necessary to observe the operational limits of the design. These limitations are set out in the "Technical Operating Specifications" volume of the Safety Analysis Report.

An exhaustive analysis is also carried out on systems Important Par Safety (IPS) to identify which equipment is required to undergo periodic testing and to justify which items do not require testing (normal operation is sufficient proof of good working order). For each system and test the "Test Procedure" document specifies the operating procedure, criteria and the required testing intervals. These instructions are used by the operators as the basis for preparing "Test Schedules".

2. Improving Safety: Operational Experience Feedback

The standardization policy adopted by EDF (one major PWR system type and a limited number of individual plant series) justifies a major commitment to maximizing the value of operational experience by placing particular emphasis on the analysis of precursor incidents. This has a dual purpose:

① to reduce the frequency of serious incidents liable to result in the generating equipment becoming unavailable, even if there is no direct bearing on safety;

② to reduce the frequency of incidents likely to have consequences to safety, in practice, the design principles for nuclear units based on Defence in Depth and the presence of barriers are such that serious accidents could only result from a simultaneous combination of independent and improbable incidents.

In terms of nuclear safety, the principal objectives of operational feedback are as follows:

① to identify precursor incidents leading to more serious accidents in order to define and implement any corrective measures required before any such accidents occur;

② to take advantage of standardized units (the generic aspects of incidents, deriving maximum benefit from modification studies, etc.);

③ to ensure, in cases where modification is necessary, that there are no adverse secondary effects before the principle is extended to the entire plant series;

④ to utilize data gathered during actual operation of the installation in order to unify the level of safety, especially in the case of a new plant series.

The guidelines on which EDF has based its operational experience feedback system are as follows:

① to systematically gather the maximum amount of data and circulate it as widely as possible, particularly within EDF;

② to bring together as many as possible designers, Operators, Manufacturers and Safety Authorities in the data analysis process;

③ to lean from experience in order to benefit not only those units planned or under construction but also units currently in service.

New Words and Expressions

facet ['fæsit]	n. 面，某一方面
insufficient [ˌinsə'fiʃənt]	adj. 不足的，不够的
specification [ˌspesifi'keiʃən]	n. 说明书；规范
periodic [ˌpiəri'ɔdik]	adj. 定期的，间发性的
interval ['intəvəl]	n. （时间的）间隔，间歇；周期
standardization [ˌstændədai'zeiʃn]	n. 标准化，标准
commitment [kə'mitmənt]	n. 交托，许诺
maximize ['mæksimaiz]	v. 把……增加（或扩大）到最大限度
precursor [pri:'kə:sə]	n. 先驱，预兆
dual ['dju:əl]	adj. 双的，二重的
unavailable [ˌʌnə'veiləbl]	adj. 无法利用的，无用的
bearing ['bɛəriŋ]	n. 关系，联系
simultaneous [ˌsaiməl'teinjəs]	adj. 同时的，一齐的
improbable [im'prɔbəbl]	adj. 不大可能（发生）的；未必会的
implement ['implimənt]	n. 贯彻，完成
corrective [kə'rektiv]	adj. 改正的，纠正的
standardize ['stændədaiz]	v. 使合标准，使标准化

generic [dʒi'nerik]	*adj.* 一般的，普通的
modification [ˌmɔdifi'keiʃən]	*n.* 修改，更改
adverse ['ædvəːs]	*adj.* 烦的，不利的，有害的
installation [ˌinstə'leiʃən]	*n.* 装置，设备
guideline ['gaidlain]	*n.* 方针，准确

Technical Terms

nuclear safety	核安全
safety level	安全水平
safety analysis	安全分析
normal operation	正常运行
test procedure	检测程序
operating procedure	操作程序
test schedule	检测时间表
operational experience feedback	操作经验反馈
generating equipment	发电设备
data analysis process	数据分析过程

Notes

1. Although the safety of a nuclear power plant is directly linked to the decision taken at the design stage and to the care taken in pre-construction studies and construction itself, it is only really in operation that nuclear safety can be seen in all its various facets, i. e. the risk of accident due to weaknesses in the design, insufficient quality or operational error.

虽然核电站的安全和设计初的决定、前期研究及建筑本身有直接的联系，但它只有在运行中才能在各个方面被发现，如由于有缺陷的设计、质量不够好或操作错误等事故风险。

2. An exhaustive analysis is also carried out on systems Important Par Safety (IPS) to identify which equipment is required to undergo periodic testing and to justify which items do not require testing (normal operation is sufficient proof of good working order).

在系统的重要组成部分安全性方面需要进行详尽的分析，确定哪些设备需要定期进行测试，哪些又是不需要测试的（正常运作已足以证明良好的工作秩序）。

Unit 2

A. Text

Biomass for Renewable Energy and Fuels

The world's energy markets rely heavily on the fossil fuels coal, petroleum crude oil, and natural gas as sources of thermal energy, gaseous, liquid, and solid fuels, and chemicals. Since millions of years are required to form fossil fuels in the earth, their reserves are finite and subject to depletion as they are consumed. The only natural, renewable carbon resource known that is large enough to be used as a substitute for fossil fuels is biomass. Included are all water- and land-based organisms, vegetation, and trees, or virgin biomass, and all dead and waste biomass such as municipal solid waste (MSW), biosolids (sewage) and animal wastes (manures) and residues, forestry and agricultural residues, and certain types of industrial wastes. Unlike fossil fuel deposits, biomass is renewable in the sense that only a short period of time is needed to replace what is used as an energy resource.

1. The Concept

The capture of solar energy as fixed carbon in biomass via photosynthesis, during which carbon dioxide (CO_2) is converted to organic compounds, is the key initial step in the growth of virgin biomass and is depicted by the following equation:

$$CO_2 + H_2O + light + chlorophyll \longrightarrow (CH_2O) + O_2 \qquad (5-1)$$

Carbohydrate, represented by the building block (CH_2O), is the primary organic product. For each gram mole of carbon fixed, about 470 kJ (112 kcal) is absorbed.

The upper limit of the capture efficiency of the incident solar radiation in biomass has been estimated to range from about 8% to as high as 15%, but under most conditions in the field, it is generally less than 2%.

The global energy potential of virgin biomass is very large. It is estimated that the world's standing terrestrial biomass carbon (i. e., the renewable, above-ground biomass that could be harvested and used as an energy resource) is approximately 100 times the world's total annual energy consumption. The largest source of standing terrestrial biomass carbon is forest biomass, which contains about 80% to 90% of the total biomass carbon. Interestingly, marine biomass carbon is projected to be next after the forest biomass carbon in terms of net annual production, but is last in terms of availability because of its high turnover rates in an oceanic environment.

2. Biomass Composition and Energy Content

With few exceptions, the order of abundance of the major organic components in whole-plant samples of terrestrial biomass is celluloses, hemicelluloses, lignins, and proteins. Aquatic biomass does not appear to follow this trend. The cellulosic components are often much lower in concentration than the hemicelluloses as illustrated by the data for water hyacinth. Other carbohydrates and derivatives are dominant in marine species such as giant brown kelp to almost complete exclusion of the celluloses. The hemicelluloses and lignins have not been found in macrocystis pyrifera.

Alpha-cellulose, or cellulose as it is more generally known, is the chief structural element and major constituent of many biomass species. In trees, it is generally about 40 to 50% of dry weight. As a general rule, the major organic components in woody biomass on a moisture and ash-free basis in weight percent are about 50 cellulosics, 25 hemicellulosics, and 25 lignins. The lipid and protein fractions of plant biomass are normally much less on a percentage basis than the carbohydrate components. The lipids are usually present at the lowest concentration, while the protein fraction is somewhat higher, but still lower than the carbohydrate fraction. Crude protein values can be approximated by multiplying the organic nitrogen analyses by 6.25. The sulfur contents of virgin and waste biomass range from very low to about 1 weight percent for primary biosolids. The sulfur content of most woody species of biomass is nil.

New Words and Expressions

depletion [diˈpliːʃən]	n.	受到损耗
natural [ˈnætʃərəl]	adj.	天然的
substitute [ˈsʌbstitjuːt]	n.	代替
vegetation [ˌvedʒiˈteiʃən]	n.	植物
biosolid [ˈbiəsɔlid]	n.	污泥
sewage [ˈsjuːidʒ]	n.	污水
manure [məˈnjuə]	n.	肥料
residue [ˈreziˌdjuː]	n.	残留物
hlorophyll [ˈklɔːrəfil]	n.	叶绿素
carbohydrate [ˈkaːbəuˈhaidreit]	n.	碳水化合物
cellulose [ˈseljuləus]	n.	纤维素
lignin [ˈlignin]	n.	木质素
protein [ˈprəutiːin]	n.	蛋白质
sulfur [ˈsʌlfə]	n.	硫
nil [nil]	n.	无，零

Technical Terms

crude oil	原油
natural gas	天然气
thermal energy	热量
municipal solid waste (MSW)	城市固体废物
animal waste	动物废料
industrial waste	工业废物
organic compound	有机化合物
carbon fixed	固定碳
solar radiation	太阳辐射

forest biomass	森林生物
marine biomass	海洋生物
turnover rate	更替率
water hyacinth	水风信子
macrocystis pyrifera	巨藻

Notes

1. The world's energy markets rely heavily on the fossil fuels coal, petroleum crude oil, and natural gas as sources of thermal energy, gaseous, liquid, and solid fuels, and chemicals.

世界能源市场严重依赖于煤，石油和天然气这些化石燃料作为热能、气体液体固体燃料和化学品的来源。

2. Carbohydrate, represented by the building block (CH_2O), is the primary organic product. For each gram mole of carbon fixed, about 470kJ (112kcal) is absorbed.

碳水化合物，CH_2O，是主要的有机产品。每摩尔固定碳，约含 470 千焦耳能量。

3. With few exceptions, the order of abundance of the major organic components in whole-plant samples of terrestrial biomass is celluloses, hemicelluloses, lignins, and proteins.

除了少数例外，陆地生物全株样本中主要有机成分从多到少顺序是纤维素、半纤维素、木质素和蛋白质。

4. The lipids are usually present at the lowest concentration, while the protein fraction is somewhat higher, but still lower than the carbohydrate fraction. Crude protein values can be approximated by multiplying the organic nitrogen analyses by 6.25.

脂类浓度通常最低，而蛋白质含量相对较高，但仍低于碳水化合物成分。粗蛋白值可用有机氮分析值乘以 6.25 来近似。

Exercises

1. Put the following phrases into English:
① 生物质　　② 植物　　③ 肥料　　④ 残留物
⑤ 光合作用　⑥ 碳水化合物　⑦ 化石燃料　⑧ 固定碳

2. Decide whether the following statements are true or false:

① The world's energy markets rely heavily on the fossil fuels coal as sources of thermal energy.

② With no exceptions, the order of abundance of the major organic components in whole-plant samples of terrestrial biomass is celluloses, hemicelluloses, lignins, and proteins.

③ The lipids are usually present at the lowest concentration, while the protein fraction is somewhat higher, but still lower than the carbohydrate fraction.

④ Alpha-cellulose, or cellulose as it is more generally known, is the chief structural element and major constituent of many biomass species. In trees, it is generally about 40% to 50% of dry weight.

B. Reading

Processes of Biomass Conversion Technologies

The technologies include a large variety of thermal and thermo-chemical processes for converting biomass by combustion, gasification, and liquefaction, and the microbial conversion of biomass to obtain gaseous and liquid fuels by fermentative methods. Examples of the former are wood-fueled power plants in which wood and wood wastes are combusted for the production of steam, which is passed through a steam turbine to generate electricity; the gasification of rice hulls by partial oxidation to yield a low-energy-value fuel gas, which drives a gas turbine to generate electric power, and finely divided silica co-product for sale; the rapid pyrolysis or thermal decomposition of wood and wood wastes to yield liquid fuel oils and chemicals; and the hydrofining of tall oils from wood pulping, vegetable oils, and waste cooking fats to obtain high-cetane diesel fuels and diesel fuel additives; examples of microbial conversion are the anaerobic digestion of biosolids to yield a relatively high-methane-content biogas of medium energy value and the alcoholic fermentation of corn to obtain fuel ethanol for use as an oxygenate and an octane-enhancing additive in motor gasolines.

Another route to liquid fuels and products is to grow certain species of biomass that serve the dual role of a carbon-fixing apparatus and a natural producer of high-energy products such as triglycerides or hydrocarbons. Examples are soybean, from which triglyceride oil coproducts are extracted and converted to biodiesel fuels, which are the transesterified methyl or ethyl esters of the fatty acid moieties of the triglycerides having cetane numbers of about 50, or the triglycerides are directly converted to high-cetane value paraffinic hydrocarbon diesel fuels having cetane numbers of about 80 to 95 by catalytic hydrogenation; the tapping of certain species of tropical trees to obtain liquid hydrocarbons suitable for use as diesel fuel without having to harvest the tree; and the extraction of terpene hydrocarbons from coniferous trees for conversion to chemicals. A multitude of processes thus exists that can be employed to obtain energy, fuels and chemicals from biomass. Many of the processes are suitable for either direct conversion of biomass or conversion of intermediates. The processes are sufficiently variable so that liquid and gaseous fuels can be produced that are identical to those obtained from fossil feedstocks, or are not identical but are suitable as fossil fuel substitutes. It is important to emphasize that virtually all of the fuels and commodity chemicals manufactured from fossil fuels can be manufactured from biomass feedstocks. Indeed, several of the processes used in a petroleum refinery for the manufacture of refined products and petrochemicals can be utilized in a biorefinery with biomass feedstocks. Note also that selected biomass feedstocks are utilized for conversion to many specialty chemicals, pharmaceuticals, natural polymers, and other higher value products.

New Words and Expressions

gasification [ˌgæsifiˈkeiʃən]	n. 气化
liquefaction [ˌlikwiˈfækʃən]	n. 液化
steam [stiːm]	n. 水蒸气
oxidation [ˌɔksiˈdeiʃən]	n. 氧化
silica [ˈsilikə]	n. 硅土，二氧化硅
pyrolysis [paiˈrɔlisis]	n. 热裂解
cetane [ˈsiːtein]	n. [化] 无色透明的饱和烃类化合物
oxygenate [ˈɔksidʒineit]	n. 含氧化合物
triglyceride [traiˈglisəraid]	n. 甘油三酯
hydrocarbon [ˈhaidrəuˌkɑːbən]	n. 烃类化合物
soybean [ˈsɔibiːn]	n. 大豆
biodiesel [bɔiˈdiːzəl]	n. 生物柴油
biorefiner [bɔi riˈfainə]	n. 生物炼制
petrochemical [ˌpetrəuˈkemikəl]	n. 石油化工产品
pharmaceutical [ˌfɑːməˈsjuːtikl]	n. 制药
polymer [ˈpɔlimə]	n. 天然聚合物

Technical Terms

thermal and thermo-chemical process	热和热化学处理
fermentative method	发酵方法
diesel fuel additive	柴油燃料添加剂
anaerobic digestion	厌氧消化
fuel ethanol	乙醇燃料
octane-enhancing additive	辛烷值增强添加剂
carbon-fixing apparatus	碳固定装置
coniferous tree	针叶树
fossil feedstock	矿物原料
methyl esters	甲基酯
ethyl esters	乙基酯
catalytic hydrogenation	催化加氢
teepee hydrocarbons	萜烯化合物

1. The technologies include a large variety of thermal and thermo-chemical processes

for converting biomass by combustion, gasification, and liquefaction, and the microbial conversion of biomass to obtain gaseous and liquid fuels by fermentative methods.

为了通过燃烧、气化、液化转化生物质能，使用的技术包括了大量的各种热和热化学转化过程，并且通过发酵方法，生物质能微生物转化以获得气体和液体燃料。

2. Another route to liquid fuels and products is to grow certain species of biomass that serve the dual role of a carbon-fixing apparatus and a natural producer of high-energy products such as triglycerides or hydrocarbons.

另一条获得液体燃料和产品的思路是种植某些生物物种，它们发挥双重作用：一个是作为碳固定装置；另一个是像甘油三酯或碳氢化合物类似的高能产品的天然生产者。

3. It is important to emphasize that virtually all of the fuels and commodity chemicals manufactured from fossil fuels can be manufactured from biomass feedstocks.

需要强调的是，事实上几乎所有从化石燃料加工而成的燃料和化学商品都可以由生物质原料制造而成。

4. Note also that selected biomass feedstocks are utilized for conversion to many specialty chemicals, pharmaceuticals, natural polymers, and other higher value products.

还要注意，所选择的生物质原料用于转换成许多特定化学品、制药、天然聚合物和其他高价值产品。

Unit 3

A. Text

Tidal Energy

Gravitational forces between the moon, the sun and the earth cause the rhythmic rising and lowering of ocean waters around the world that result in Tide Waves. The moon exerts more than twice as great a force on the tides as the sun due to its much closer position to the earth. As a result, the tide closely follows the moon during its rotation around the earth, creating diurnal tide and ebb cycles at any particular ocean surface. The amplitude or height of the tide wave is very small in the open ocean where it measures several centimeters in the center of the wave distributed over hundreds of kilometers. However, the tide can increase dramatically when it reaches continental shelves, bringing huge masses of water into narrow bays and river estuaries along a coastline. For instance, the tides in the Bay of Fundy in Canada are the greatest in the world, with amplitude between 16 and 17 meters near shore. High tides close to these figures can be observed at many other sites worldwide, such as the Bristol Channel in England, the Kimberly coast of Australia, and the Okhotsk Sea of Russia. Table 5-1 contains ranges of amplitude for some locations with large tides.

Table 5-1 Highest tides (tide ranges) of the global ocean

Country	Site	Tide range/m
Canada	Bay of Fundy	16.2
England	Severn Estuary	14.5
France	Port of Ganville	14.7
France	La Rance	13.5
Argentina	Puerto Rio Gallegos	13.3
Russia	Bay of Mezen(White Sea)	10.0
Russia	Penzhinskaya Guba(Sea of Okhotsk)	13.4

On most coasts tidal fluctuation consists of two floods and two ebbs, with a semidiurnal period of about 12 hours and 25 minutes. However, there are some coasts where tides are twice as long (diurnal tides) or are mixed, with a diurnal inequality, but are still diurnal or semidiurnal in period. The magnitude of tides changes during each lunar month. The highest tides, called spring tides, occur when the moon, earth and sun are positioned close to a straight line (moon syzygy). The lowest tides, called neap tides, occur when the earth, moon and sun are at right angles to each other (moon quadrature). Isaac Newton formulated the phenomenon first as follows: "the ocean must flow twice and ebb twice, each day, and the highest water occurs at third hour after the approach of the luminaries to the meridian of the place". The tidal amplitudes were published by the British Admiralty in 1833. However, information about tide fluctuations was available long before that time from a fourteenth century British atlas, for example.

Rising and receding tides along a shoreline area can be explained in the following way. A low height tide wave of hundreds of kilometers in diameter runs on the ocean surface under the moon, following its rotation around the earth, until the wave hits a continental shore. The water mass moved by the moon's gravitational pull fills narrow bays and river estuaries where it has no way to escape and spread over the ocean. This leads to interference of waves and accumulation of water inside these bays and estuaries, resulting in dramatic rises of the water level (tide cycle). The tide starts receding as the moon continues its travel further over the land, away from the ocean, reducing its gravitational influence on the ocean waters (ebb cycle).

The above explanation is rather schematic since only the moon's gravitation has been taken into account as the major factor influencing tide fluctuations. Other factors, which affect the tide rang are the sun's pull, the centrifugal force resulting from the earth's rotation and, in some cases, local resonance of the gulfs, bays or estuaries.

New Words and Expressions

rhythmic ['riðmik] 　　　　　　　　　n. 有节奏的；有韵律的

diurnal [daiˈəːnəl]	adj.	每天的
centimeter [ˈsentimiːtər]	n.	厘米
coastline [ˈkəustˌlain]	n.	海岸线
inequality [ˌiniˈkwɔlitiː]	n.	不平衡
estuary [ˈestʃuːeriː]	n.	（江河入海的）河口，河口湾，港湾

Technical Terms

gravitational force	引力
ebb cycle	潮汐周期
continental shelf	大陆架
semidiurnal period	半日周期
lunar month	农历月
gravitational pull	万有引力
centrifugal force	离心力
local resonance	局部共振

Notes

1. Bay of Fundy 芬迪湾

2. Bristol Channel 布里斯托尔频道

3. Okhotsk Sea 鄂霍次克海

4. moon syzygy 对点；会合；朔望（指日、月、地球约略成一直线）

5. moon quadrature 月亮角度正交。在农历初七和二十二左右，地球、太阳、月球形成直角，由于太阳和月亮对地球潮汐的影响部分抵消，所产生的潮汐高度也较低，称为小潮。

6. The moon exerts more than twice as great a force on the tides as the sun due to its much closer position to the earth. As a result, the tide closely follows the moon during its rotation around the earth, creating diurnal tide and ebb cycles at any particular ocean surface.

由于月亮距离地球更近，其施加给地球潮汐的力量超过太阳所施加的两倍以上。因此，潮水紧跟着在地球周围旋转的月球运动，在任何特定的海洋表面产生了潮涨潮落周期。

7. On most coasts tidal fluctuation consists of two floods and two ebbs, with a semidiurnal period of about 12 hours and 25 minutes. However, there are some coasts where tides are twice as long (diurnal tides) or are mixed, with a diurnal inequality, but are still diurnal or semidiurnal in period. The magnitude of tides changes during each lunar month. The highest tides, called spring tides, occur when the moon, earth and sun are positioned close to a straight line.

在大多数海岸，潮汐波动包括两个潮涨潮落，即半日周期约 12 小时 25 分钟。然而，有一些海岸，潮汐时间是半日潮的两倍或者是混合着一日潮，但总归是半日或者一日潮。潮汐的规模在每一个农历月变化。最高潮汐，称为大潮，在月亮、地球和太阳的位置接近一条直线时发生。

8. A low height tide wave of hundreds of kilometers in diameter runs on the ocean surface under the moon, following its rotation around the earth, until the wave hits a continental shore.

数百公里直径的低高度潮汐波浪在月亮的作用下，在地球海洋表面上运动，直到浪潮打击到陆地海岸。

9. The tide starts receding as the moon continues its travel further over the land, away from the ocean, reducing its gravitational influence on the ocean waters.

当月亮继续进一步按自己的轨道行走时，浪潮开始后退，远离海洋，减少它对海洋水域的引力作用。

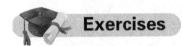

Exercises

1. Put the following phrases into English:
① 万有引力　② 潮汐　③ 大陆架　④ 海岸线
⑤ 农历　⑥ 港湾　⑦ 月亮角度正交　⑧ 局部共振

2. Decide whether the following statements are true or false:

① The moon exerts more than twice as great a force on the tides as the sun due to its much closer position to the earth.

② On all coasts tidal fluctuation consists of two floods and two ebbs, with a semidiurnal period of about 12 hours and 25 minutes.

③ The magnitude of tides changes during each lunar month.

④ The amplitude or height of the tide wave is very small in the open ocean where it measures several centimeters in the center of the wave distributed over hundreds of kilometers.

B. Reading

Utilizing Electric Energy from Tidal Power Plants

A serious issue that must be addressed is how and where to use the electric power generated by extracting energy from the tides. Tides are cyclical by their nature, and the corresponding power output of a tidal power plant does not always coincide with the peak of human activity. In countries with a well-developed power industry, tidal power plants can be a part of the general power distribution system. However, power from a tidal plant would then have to be transmitted a long distance because locations of high tides are usually far away from industrial and urban centers. An attractive future option is to utilize the tidal power in situ for year-round production of hydrogen fuel by electrolysis of the water.

The hydrogen, liquefied or stored by another method, can be transported or stored by another method, can be transported anywhere to be used either as a fuel instead of oil or gasoline or in various fuel cell energy systems. Fuel cells convert hydrogen energy directly into electricity without combustion or moving parts, which is then used, for instance, in electric cars. Many scientists and engineers consider such a development as a future new industrial revolution. However, in order to realize this idea worldwide, clean hydrogen fuel would need to be also available everywhere.

At present most hydrogen is produced from natural gases and fossil fuels, which emit greenhouse gases into the atmosphere and harm the global ecosystem. From this point of view, production of hydrogen by water electrolysis using tidal energy is one of the best ways to develop clean hydrogen fuel by a clean method. Thus, tidal energy can be used in the future to help develop a new era of clean industries, for example, to clean up the automotive industry, as well as other energy-consuming areas of human activity.

New Words and Expressions

coincide [ˌkəuinˈsaid]	v. 与……一致；想法、意见等相同；相符
transmit [trænzˈmit]	v. 传输；传送，发射，发送信号
attractive [əˈtræktiv]	adj. 有魅力的；引人注目的；迷人的
hydrogen [ˈhaidrədʒən]	n. 氢
liquefy [ˈlikwəfai]	v. 液化，溶解
ecosystem [ˈekəuˌsistəm]	n. 生态系统
in situ	在原位，在原处

Technical Terms

power distribution system	电源分配系统
hydrogen fuel	氢燃料
electrolysis of the water	电解水
fuel cell	燃料电池

Notes

1. A serious issue that must be addressed is how and where to use the electric power generated by extracting energy from the tides.
一个必须解决的严重问题是如何和在哪里使用由潮汐提取的能量所产生的电力。

2. In countries with a well-developed power industry, tidal power plants can be a part of the general power distribution system. However, power from a tidal plant would then have to be transmitted a long distance because locations of high tides are usually far away

from industrial and urban centers.

在能量产业发展不错的国家，潮汐发电厂可以成为总配电系统的一个部分。然而，从潮汐电站所发电能必须远距离传输，这是由于高位潮汐的位置通常远离工业和城市中心。

3. The hydrogen, liquefied or stored by another method, can be transported or stored by another method, can be transported anywhere to be used either as a fuel instead of oil or gasoline or in various fuel cell energy systems.

液化氢或者另一种方式存储的氢，可以运输或者以另一种方法储存，它可以运输到任何地方，代替石油或汽油用作燃料，或者用在各种燃料电池能量系统当中。

Unit 4

A. Text

Geothermal Energy—A Quick Look

Figure 5-1　A volcanic eruption

Anyone old enough to get their head around a volcanic eruption (Figure 5-1) understands that inside the planet Earth things are pretty warm. And we've all seen images, or been lucky enough to see in person, the eruption of geysers. The reason for these events is heat and pressure from below the Earth's surface. The heat is partly left over from the formation of the planet billions of years ago, but mostly from radioactive decay at the Earth's core. This is a natural process that produces heat energy. A lot of heat energy. Enough to melt rock, hence the lava flows you see coming out of volcanoes from time to time.

So the geothermal technology is the use of that heat, sometimes directly, mostly indirectly. There are small-scale residential products, and there are huge industrial and utility provider projects (Figure 5-2) tapping deep into the Earth. Over 70 countries now use some kind of geothermal electrical generation on a commercial scale.

The International Geothermal Association (IGA) monitors the continual growth of worldwide geothermal installations. They are represented by over 5,200 members in nearly 70 countries. They report huge growth in geothermal installations worldwide over the last 2 decades as the technology for getting to the heat & bringing it back has improved.

Figure 5-2　An industrial geothermal product

So the first challenge is the expense of deep drilling to get to the heat source. The second challenge is having enough liquid locally to drive to the heat source to "collect" the heat energy and bring it back to where it can be used at the surface.

To put the drilling in perspective, hot dry rock (HDR) projects typically require 2 holes (Figure 5-3) to be bored. The first allows the injection of cold water from the surface to the hot rock area, which causes heat-stress cracks in the rocks and creates a hot "reservoir". A second hole is drilled to allow the extraction of the heated water (now steam) up to the surface where its heat energy is used to drive turbines and create electricity. There is a European HDR project in France that has a bore depth of over 16,000 feet.

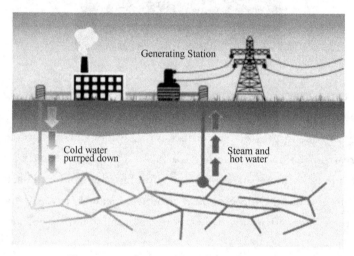

Figure 5-3　A typical hot dry rock solution

In California geothermal fields known as The Geysers were dry and unusable at the end of the 1980's, despite plenty of heat available. The solution in 1997 was to pump treated waste-water about 30 miles to the project and then down to the heat. After this success the Santa Rosa Geysers used the same concept, moving around 11 million gallons per day of treated waste-water over 40 miles and down to the hot rocks.

As we get more creative with our solutions to the challenges of sing heat from inside the earth, prices will continue to fall and geothermal solutions will become an ever more important aspect of out planet's alternative energy solutions.

New Words and Expressions

pretty ['priti]	*adv.*	相当，颇
geyser ['giːzə(r)]	*n.*	间歇岩
lava ['lɑːvə]	*n.*	熔岩，火山岩
injection [in'dʒekʃn]	*n.*	注射
crack [kræk]	*n.*	裂纹
reservoir ['rezəvwɑː(r)]	*n.*	水库，储藏
volcanic eruption		火山爆发
in person		亲自，亲身

Technical Terms

radioactive decay	放射性衰变
geothermal installation	地热安装
International Geothermal Association (IGA)	国际地热协会
hot dry rock (HDR)	干热岩

Notes

1. Anyone old enough to get their head around a volcanic eruption understands that inside the planet Earth things are pretty warm.
任何成年人都可以由火山爆发明白地球里面是很温暖的。

2. They report huge growth in geothermal installations worldwide over the last 2 decades as the technology for getting to the heat & bringing it back has improved.
他们报告了在过去20年里随着从地下获得地热及带其回到地表的技术改进后全球地热安装的巨大增长。

3. The first allows the injection of cold water from the surface to the hot rock area, which causes heat-stress cracks in the rocks and creates a hot "reservoir". A second hole is drilled to allow the extraction of the heated water (now steam) up to the surface where its heat energy is used to drive turbines and create electricity.
第一个洞从地球表面向热岩区注入冷水，造成岩石中的热应力裂缝，并创建一个热的"水库"。第二个洞里允许将热水（现为蒸汽）提取至地表面，用来驱动涡轮机产生电能。

4. After this success the Santa Rosa Geysers used the same concept, moving around 11 million gallons per day of treated waste-water over 40 miles and down to the hot rocks.
在这一成功后，圣塔罗萨间歇泉使用同样的概念，每天移动大约1100万加仑的废水至地下超过40英里到地热岩石。

5. As we get more creative with our solutions to the challenges of sing heat from inside the earth, prices will continue to fall and geothermal solutions will become an ever more important aspect of out planet's alternative energy solutions.

当我们面对获取来自地球内部热能的挑战变得更有创造力时，其价格将继续下降，地热将成为这个星球的替代能源解决方案中一个越来越重要的方面。

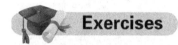

Exercises

1. Put the following phrases into English:
① 火山爆发　　② 放射性衰变　　③ 间歇岩
④ 注射　　　　⑤ 水库　　　　　⑥ 裂纹

2. Decide whether the following statements are true or false:
① To put the drilling in perspective, hot dry rock projects typically require 2 holes to be bored.
② The solution in 1997 was to pump treated waste-water about 300 miles to the project and then down to the heat.
③ The geothermal technology is the use of that heat directly.

3. Translating:
① The heat is partly left over from the formation of the planet billions of years ago, but mostly from radioactive decay at the Earth's core.
② The solution in 1997 was to pump treated waste-water about 30 miles to the project and then down to the heat.

B. Reading

10 Reasons Why We Should Use Geothermal Energy

Awareness of the environmental drawbacks of fossil fuels—coal, oil and natural gasis on the rise. So is interest in eco-friendly alternatives for meeting society's energy needs. Although fossil fuels generally remain abundant and cheap, rival energies have gained traction in recent years amid an unprecedented wave of green investments.

The most promising one among the rising green stars is geothermal energy (Figure 5-4). The advantages linked to this abundant subterranean resource are many. Check out our list of the top ten reasons we should consider a future in which geothermal energy figures prominently.

1. 100% Renewable

Geothermal power is based on heat energy stored underneath the ground. This intense heat is trapped in enormous quantities inside water reservoirs in the earth's crust. In fact, it is considered essentially limitless.

2. Clean-Burning and Low-Emission

Figure 5-4 Geothermal energy

Geothermal energy is considered clean because it can be extracted and converted without burning any fossil fuels. The "emissions" from a geothermal plant are mainly benign water vapors.

3. High Energy Potential

Oil and other "fossil" fuels are just that—finite fossils that took a long time to form millions of years ago. As a result, there is only so much valuable oil we can extract form identified reserves. At some point, it could simply become cost-ineffective to drill for what's left of the world's petroleum—not to mention prohibitively destructive of the global climate. Geothermal resources have astonishing energy potential by comparison, estimated at 2 terawatts globally—about 15,000 times more than estimated worldwide oil reserves.

4. Scalable Production

Some level of geothermal energy is available in most places. There is potential for geothermal development throughout the United States, and the process is highly scalable.

5. Base Load Stability

Unlike renewables such as solar and wind power, geothermal energy maintains an ideal stability night and day, regardless of lighting and wind conditions. That makes it eligible to supply base load electricity to the grid.

6. Light on Carbon

A geothermal system is an excellent way to substantially reduce a building's carbon footprint. Zoe Reich, an environmental specialist with engineering firm Edwards & Zuck, says a correctly installed geothermal pump system can shave a building's utility costs by up to 60 percent. While geothermal energy is not entirely carbon-free, it releases a fraction as much carbon dioxide into the atmosphere as fossil fuels. Additionally, power is generated on-site at geothermal plants, saving the costly energy associated with transporting and processing pricey fuels.

7. Low-Maintenance versatility

Geothermal energy can replace both heating and cooling systems in buildings—and do both jobs more efficiently than conventional air-cooled systems. Why? Subsurface temperatures remain constant year-round. Moreover, the elegant operational simplicity of a typical system and the absence of carbon fouling due to combustion mean geothermal systems are easy to maintain.

8. Smart Land Use

Geothermal energy has the smallest land footprint of any major power source. It doesn't require much additional real estate—a boon in dense urban zones. Additionally, underground geothermal systems aren't exposed to the elements. This is important during extreme weather as it protects crucial energy supplies from natural disasters that threaten aboveground units.

9. Green Economy

The uncapped energy potential of hydrothermal reservoirs means there will never be anything like "peak geothermal". This has serious implications for job creation and the strength of the green economy. It takes a lot of workers to build and run geothermal power plants. Each phase of development represents valuable jobs for electricians, pipefitters, engineers, recruits from top geology programs, and more.

10. Promising Technologies

While geothermal production has its own exploration risks and cost foibles, its product research risk is less than in many other renewable energy industries. And now, emerging technologies could let engineers use lower temperatures and drill deeper, potentially expanding access to geothermal power in more locations. The long-term outlook for this plentiful source of clean energy is quite bright.

New Words and Expressions

eco-friendly [ˌiːkəˈfrendli]	adj.	对生态环境友好的，不妨害生态环境的
subterranean [ˌsʌbtəˈreiniən]	adj.	地表下面的，地下的，隐藏的
crust [krʌst]	n.	外壳，地壳
benign [biˈnain]	adj.	温和的，有利于健康的
prohibitively [prəʊˈhibitivli]	adv.	禁止地，非常地
destructive [diˈstrʌktiv]	adj.	破坏性的，毁灭性的，有害的
eligible [ˈelidʒəbl]	adj.	合适的，合格的
boon [buːn]	n.	恩惠，福利
pipefitter [ˈpaipfitə]	n.	管道工，管子工
recruit [riˈkruːt]	n.	新兵，新成员

Part V Other New Energy

Technical Terms

scalable production   可扩展生产
base load   基本负荷

Notes

1. Awareness of the environmental drawbacks of fossil fuels—coal, oil and natural gas—is on the rise. So is interest in eco-friendly alternatives for meeting society's energy needs.

对于如煤炭、石油和天然气之类化石燃料的环境问题的警觉正在逐渐上升,为满足社会能源的需要,对于环保替代品的兴趣也是如此。

2. Geothermal resources have astonishing energy potential by comparison, estimated at 2 terawatts globally—about 15,000 times more than estimated worldwide oil reserves.

地热资源相比较而言有惊人的能源潜力,估计在全球范围内有超过 2 太瓦的热能,是全世界石油储量的 15000 倍。

3. While geothermal energy is not entirely carbon-free, it releases a fraction as much carbon dioxide into the atmosphere as fossil fuels. Additionally, power is generated on-site at geothermal plants, saving the costly energy associated with transporting and processing pricey fuels.

然而地热能源不是完全的无碳排放,它释放的二氧化碳相当于化石燃料释放的很小一部分。此外,在地热发电厂发电是现场的,节省昂贵的需要运输和处理的能源。

4. And now, emerging technologies could let engineers use lower temperatures and drill deeper, potentially expanding access to geothermal power in more locations.

现在,新兴技术可以让工程师使用更低的温度钻得更深,有可能在更多的位置扩大开发地热发电。

Unit 5

A. Text

Hydro Power—Time to Dive In

1. Hydro-electric Power

"Hydro" or water power refers to the energy of the movement of water being converted into electricity (Figure 5-5), hence the more common term "hydro-electric power". You've probably heard of, or even visited, the Hoover Dam. So as long as we have moving water we will have access to a sustainable and renewable energy source. But there are many ways to utilize the energy of our waters to create useable electricity. Here we'll in-

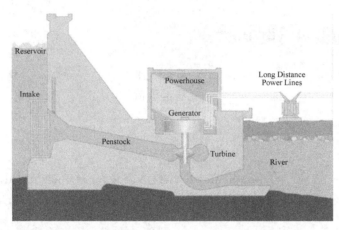

Figure 5-5　Hydroelectric dam

troduce some of the ideas currently being used or researched in the general field of Hydro Power.

2. Ocean Power

First up is Ocean Power, often called marine power. The moon's gravitational pull as it revolves around us, and the sun's as we revolve around it, create the high and low tides around the world. This, combined with local weather patterns and ocean currents, creates huge movements of water which harness incredible amounts of kinetic energy. Ocean power is the phrase associated with capturing some of this energy and converting it into useable electrical power.

3. Current Power

Or Ocean Current Power—who hasn't heard of the Gulf Stream? —This is a flow of water so immense that it is bigger than the flow of every river on the planet combined. If we could capture just 20% of its energy we could power the entire USA. Such technology is still in its infancy, and is largely based around turbine principals similar in concept to wind-turbines, but designed and engineered to live underwater.

4. Wave Power

More specifically, wave power refers to the kinetic energy in ocean waves and its use either to drive turbines for electrical generation, or put to other mechanical uses such as pumping stations.

5. Osmotic Power

This concept seems the most like science fiction of the various hydro-powers. However, it is a process which has virtually no fuel cost, and emits no noxious gases into our atmosphere. The idea is to extract energy from the difference in salinity between fresh water and sea water through the process of osmosis. A test plant has been constructed in Norway and has shown good early results—albeit on a small scale of just a few kW—and plans are being developed for a large scale commercial osmotic power plant right now.

6. Tidal Power

Still in research and development phases the idea is to capture incoming tidewaters in lakes and as the tide goes out the water is channeled to drive turbines. Advances in turbine technology are opening up new opportunities to exploit tidal energies, which are easier to plan for than the more weather-related wave energies.

7. Low Head Hydro Power (Figure 5-6)

Figure 5-6 Low head hydro power

Unlike at the Hoover Dam Power Plant which uses a "high" head of pressure, there are opportunities for smaller scale power plants along less dramatic rivers. This uses "low head" or "dam-less" river flows, usually with a smaller waterfall, and a hydro-kinetic turbine. This special turbine can take advantage of the natural flow of a river and provide smaller amounts of electricity to local users or into the main power grid.

So there's a lot going on in the world of hydro-power. Without a doubt it's an area of massive energy supply that our current technology has barely-tapped, but is getting better every day.

New Words and Expressions

sustainable [sə'steinəbl]　　　　*adj.* 可持续的
harness ['haːnis]　　　　　　　*v.* 利用，控制
mechanical [mə'kænikl]　　　　*adj.* 机械的
salinity [sə'linəti]　　　　　　　*n.* 盐度
albeit [ɔːl'biːit]　　　　　　　　*conj.* 虽然，尽管

Technical Terms

kinetic energy　　　　　　　　动能
noxious gas　　　　　　　　　有害气体

osmotic power	渗透发电
hydro-electric power	水力发电
marine power	海洋发电
low head hydro power	低水头水电

Notes

1. Hoover Dam 美国胡佛大坝
2. Gulf Stream 墨西哥湾流
3. The moon's gravitational pull as it revolves around us, and the sun's as we revolve around it, create the high and low tides around the world.

月球围绕着我们，我们围绕着太阳，相互之间存在着引力，产生围绕着地球的或高或低的潮汐。

4. This is a flow of water so immense that it is bigger than the flow of every river on the planet combined.

这个湾流的水流是如此巨大，比地球上所有河流水流的总和都大。

5. A test plant has been constructed in Norway and has shown good early results—albeit on a small scale of just a few kW—and plans are being developed for a large scale commercial osmotic power plant right now.

一个试验厂已在挪威建成并表现出良好的早期结果——虽然规模很小只有几千瓦，现在正计划开发一个大型的商业渗透电厂。

6. Advances in turbine technology are opening up new opportunities to exploit tidal energies, which are easier to plan for than the more weather-related wave energies.

涡轮技术的进步正在给开发潮汐能提供新的机遇，这比与天气相关的波能要容易计划。

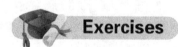
Exercises

1. Put the following phrases into English:
① 利用　　② 盐度　　③ 潮汐
④ 动能　　⑤ 水力发电　　⑥ 引力

2. Decide whether the following statements are true or false:

① The Gulf Stream is a flow of water so immense that it is bigger than the flow of every river on the planet combined.

② The low head hydro power uses "low head" or "dam-less" river flows, usually with a smaller waterfall, and a hydro-kinetic turbine.

③ As long as we have much water we will have access to a sustainable and renewable energy source.

3. **Translate the following sentences:**

① More specifically, wave power refers to the kinetic energy in ocean waves and its use either to drive turbines for electrical generation, or put to other mechanical uses such as pumping stations.

② This uses "low head" or "dam-less" river flows, usually with a smaller waterfall, and a hydro-kinetic turbine.

B. Reading

Ocean Currents—Harnessing the Power

A small cog in the worldwide colossus Siemens AG is a company called Marine Current Turbines, or MCT. They are part of Siemens' Ocean & Hydro Business division, and are at the front line of ocean power technology development. Remarkably, they've been at this for over 2 decades.

The more accurate term for this technology is Tidal Stream Energy Generation, and MCT have demonstrated the technology on a large enough scale to present it as a feasible commercial solution (Figure 5-7). They're ready for business.

Figure 5-7 A marine current turbine

The company is underway already on initial developments off the coast of Bristol in SW England. The project is enthusiastically supported by local government officials and Members of Parliament, who are actively reviewing an entire Energy Manifesto for SW England.

MCT is the world's leader in tidal stream energy technology, and since their acquisition by Siemens in 2012 they now have the financial muscle to make major marine energy projects happen.

So what exactly is "tidal energy" and how can we use it?

The moon (and to a lesser degree the sun) creates tidal effects in the planet's oceans.

These tides are very predictable and can therefore be utilized to create reliable, consistent electricity generation from a genuinely renewable and sustainable source. The technology calls for huge turbines to be installed on the sea-bed in the line of the tidal currents. The huge forces of the fast moving water drive the turbines and then create electricity for the main power grid.

The equipment used looks like something from a science fiction movie, and is in itself an amazing engineering feat. The force of the water flow is powerful, very powerful. In the UK operation the energy of the flow is equal to winds in excess of 300mph. To put this in perspective, a category 5 super-hurricane has wind speeds above 157mph, so the tidal energies available are shockingly big. This is because of the much greater density of water vs. air, so more energy is available as much lower flow speeds. The machinery is called SeaGen (Figure 5-8), and several work together to "farm" the sea's tidal energy.

Figure 5-8　SeaGen

The SeaGen equipment is designed to handle these forces & convert them into electricity for the grid. And the UK, in a prime geographical position because of the Gulf Stream is poised to dominate the tidal energy business for Europe, with MCT leading the way.

 New Words and Expressions

cog [kɔg]	n.	齿轮，钝齿，雄榫
colossus [kəˈlɔsəs]	n.	巨像，巨人，大国，大企业
feasible [ˈfiːzəbl]	adj.	可行的，可用的，可实行的
underway [ˌʌndəˈwei]	adj.	在进行中的，起步的
enthusiastically [inˌθjuːziˈæstikli]	adv.	热心地，满腔热情地，起劲
manifesto [ˌmæniˈfestəu]	n.	宣言，声明，告示
acquisition [ˌækwiˈziʃn]	n.	获得，取得
genuinely [ˈdʒenjuinli]	adv.	真正地，真诚地，诚实地
feat [fiːt]	n.	功绩，伟业，卓绝的手艺，技术

machinery [məʃiːnəri]　　　　　　　　　n. （总称）机器，机器的运转部分，机械装置
Member of Parliament　　　　　　　　下议院议员

Technical Terms

Marine Current Turbines　　　　　　　简称 MCT，洋流涡轮机（公司名）
Tidal Stream Energy Generation　　　　潮流能发电

Notes

1. Siemens AG 西门子股份公司，AG 是德语里 Aktien Gesellschaft 的缩写，与英文中 joint stock company 意同，即股份公司。

2. SeaGen 一种新型潮汐能涡轮发电机，是彼得·弗伦克尔工程师的设想和不懈努力的结果。

3. The company is underway already on initial developments off the coast of Bristol in SW England. The project is enthusiastically supported by local government officials and Members of Parliament, who are actively reviewing an entire Energy Manifesto for SW England.

公司已经在位于英格兰西南部的布里斯托尔海岸初步开展工作。该项目得到当地政府官员和议会议员的热情支持，这些人正积极重新审视英格兰西南部的整个能量宣言。

4. The force of the water flow is powerful, very powerful. In the UK operation the energy of the flow is equal to winds in excess of 300mph.

水流的力量是强大的，非常强大。在英国，实际操作中，水流的能量与超过 300 英里/时的大风相对等。

5. To put this in perspective, a category 5 super-hurricane has wind speeds above 157mph, so the tidal energies available are shockingly big.

准确的说，一个超 5 类飓风风速高于 157 英里/时，所以说潮汐的能量很大（大约 300 英里/时）。

Part Ⅵ New Application

Unit 1

A. Text

A Solar Powered Ship. Wow!

Tûranor PlanetSolar, the world's largest (so far) solar powered vessel (Figure 6-1), put to sea on March 31 2010 and achieved 3 record breaking feats:

Figure 6-1 Tûranor PlanetSolar

① She became the first ship relying entirely on solar energy to circumnavigate the planet, an astonishing 37,000 mile journey taking some 19 months.

② She achieved the fasted crossing of the Atlantic Ocean by a solar vessel.

③ She took the record for the longest distance covered by an electric vehicle of any kind.

In May 2013 PlanetSolar broke its own transatlantic record, making the crossing in just 22 days. And this is a nice looking ship. At over 100 feet in length, the longer term plan is for the boat to possibly be used as a charter yacht—albeit a high end luxury charter. For now, it has become a scientific research ship, moving up the Gulf Stream off the Eastern US seaboard, then across the Atlantic to Norway. Researchers on board are examining the effects of aerosols in the atmosphere, and other climate related issues.

The solar panels, comprising some 38,000 solar cells, produce over 90kW of energy—enough for 7 or 8 average sized homes. The panels charge a huge bank of lithium-ion batteries stored in the hulls of the catamaran, which add over 8 tons of ballast, and can push PlanetSolar along at an impressive 14 knots (Figure 6-2).

Figure 6-2 Tûranor PlanetSolar is fast moving

Commonly referred to as PlanetSolar, the first part of the name, Tûranor, comes from Tolkien's Lord of the Rings, and is given the meaning "the power of the sun". The $16.5 million construction of the ship was funded by a German entrepreneur, and has an international crew of 6.

This amazing venture is aimed at promoting awareness globally of protecting our environment by the use of renewable energy sources.

Captain Gérard d'Aboville faces a different navigational challenge than that of other boat captains—the sun is his constant pursuit. An occasional cloudy day is not a major issue, since they can cruise for up to 3 days on the batteries' charge. But the challenge is constant to keep the batteries at optimum charge, so a detour is sometimes necessary to avoid inclement weather. "I have this new parameter of the sun" he said, "and it makes life interesting."

New Words and Expressions

circumnavigate [ˌsəːkəmˈnævigeit]　　　v. 环航
planet [ˈplænit]　　　n. 行星，星相
astonishing [əˈstɒniʃiŋ]　　　adj. 使人吃惊的，惊人的
vessel [ˈvesl]　　　n. 容器；船，飞船
transatlantic [ˌtrænzətˈlæntik]　　　adj. 横跨大西洋的，美国的
yacht [jɒt]　　　n. 快艇，帆船，游艇
aerosol [ˈeərəsɔːl, -ˌsɒl]　　　n. 气溶胶
ballast [ˈbæləst]　　　n. 镇流器
knot [nɒt]　　　n. 节（航海用）
entrepreneur [ˌɒntrəprəˈnɜː(r)]　　　n. 企业家

cruise [kru:z]　　　　　　　　　v. 巡航
detour ['di:tuə (r)]　　　　　　n. 车辆绕行
the Atlantic Ocean　　　　　　大西洋
in the hulls of the catamaran　在双体船的船体

Technical Terms

lithium-ion battery　　　　　　锂离子电池
at optimum charge　　　　　　 处于最佳负荷

Notes

1. She became the first ship relying entirely on solar energy to circumnavigate the planet, an astonishing 37,000 mile journey taking some 19 months.

她成为完全依靠太阳能环绕地球的第一艘轮船，令人惊奇地花了19个月航行37000英里旅程。

2. For now, it has become a scientific research ship, moving up the Gulf Stream off the Eastern US seaboard, then across the Atlantic to Norway.

现在，它已成为一个科学研究的轮船，沿着墨西哥湾流从美国东海岸驶出，然后横跨大西洋到挪威。

3. The panels charge a huge bank of lithium-ion batteries stored in the hulls of the catamaran, which add over 8 tons of ballast, and can push PlanetSolar along at an impressive 14 knots.

这些面板对位于双体船的船体上的巨大锂离子电池充电，增加了超过8吨的镇流器，能够以令人惊奇的14海里/小时的速度推动船体前行。

4. This amazing venture is aimed at promoting awareness globally of protecting our environment by the use of renewable energy sources.

这个惊人的冒险旨在促进通过使用可再生能源来保护环境的意识。

5. An occasional cloudy day is not a major issue, since they can cruise for up to 3 days on the batteries' charge.

偶尔阴天不是一个大问题，因为他们可以使用电池航船3天。

Exercises

1. Put the following phrases into English:
① 锂电池　　② 大西洋　　③ 双体船
④ 环航　　　⑤ 游艇　　　⑥ 巡航

2. Decide whether the following statements are true or false:
① Tûranor PlanetSolar is the largest solar powered vessel of the world.

② Tûranor PlanetSolar took the record for the longest distance covered by an electric vehicle of any kind.

③ The ship was funded by a German entrepreneur in order to make money.

④ The ship cannot work in an occasional cloudy or rainy day.

3. Translate the following sentences:

① At over 100 feet in length, the longer term plan is for the boat to possibly be used as a charter yacht—albeit a high end luxury charter.

② The solar panels, comprising some 38,000 solar cells, produce over 90kW of energy—enough for 7 or 8 average sized homes.

③ But the challenge is constant to keep the batteries at optimum charge, so a detour is sometimes necessary to avoid inclement weather. "I have this new parameter of the sun," he said, "and it makes life interesting."

B. Reading

Solar Mobile Charging Stations—Thanks to Super Storm Sandy!

As reported by Reuters, AT&T has sponsored the installation of the first 25 solar powered mobile device charging stations (Figure 6-3) in New York. This is a rare but growing phenomenon—public demand to resolve an issue results in a 'green' solution, rather than a knee-jerk partisan political reaction.

Figure 6-3 Solar mobile charging station

Super Storm Sandy passed through several North East States, including New York, thrashing the region severely and leaving millions without power—almost a million in New York alone. The October 2012 storm delivered a record setting 14 foot sea surge into downtown Manhattan, causing billions of dollars in damage, and would be responsible for taking over 130 lives.

In such extreme circumstances, communication is vital. Today's reality is that our mobile devices have become an intricate part of our daily lives, so to suddenly not be able to charge them in order to make an urgent phone call was a huge issue for many. People were walking long distances and waiting in long queues just to charge a cell phone.

The city of New York responded quickly, setting up temporary street-based charging systems in key locations badly affected by the storm. This relatively simple act has developed into the addition of permanent outdoor charging stations.

Each system is powered by a large battery bank which is charged every day using solar power. Sponsored by AT&T, each station has six docks with a selection of power outlet options to charge phones, tablets and even laptops. The clever design will reserve enough power to keep charging mobile devices on shady days and at night.

AT&T is footing the bill entirely for the setup and maintenance, the city of New York is simply providing the locations, another coup for New York Mayor Michael Bloomberg, and a nice advertising opportunity for AT&T!

The first 25 stations will be distributed around the city's 5 boroughs, an idea that is sure to spread to other cities in the near future, so watch out for a mobile charging station near you soon.

New Words and Expressions

knee-jerk [niːdʒɜːk]	adj.	下意识的
partisan [ˌpɑːtiˈzæn]	adj.	党派的
thrash [θræʃ]	v.	鞭打
vital [ˈvaitl]	adj.	至关重要的
intricate [ˈintrikət]	adj.	错综复杂的
coup [kuː]	n.	政变，机敏的策略
AT&T	abbr.	American Telephone & Telegraph Co. 美国电话电报公司
Super Storm Sandy		飓风桑迪

Technical Terms

solar mobile charging station　　　　　　　太阳能手机充电站

Notes

1. This is a rare but growing phenomenon—public demand to resolve an issue results in a "green" solution, rather than a knee-jerk partisan political reaction.

这是一种罕见但又逐渐增多的现象：公共需求用一种"绿色"的方式解决问题，而不是一种本能的党派政治反应。

2. Today's reality is that our mobile devices have become an intricate part of our daily lives, so to suddenly not be able to charge them in order to make an urgent phone call was

a huge issue for many.

现在的实际情况是我们的移动设备已经成为我们日常生活中一个复杂的部分,以致突然不能充电拨打紧急电话对很多人来说是个大问题。

3. Sponsored by AT&T, each station has six docks with a selection of power outlet options to charge phones, tablets and even laptops.

由 AT&T 公司赞助,每站都有六个区配有电源选项来对手机、平板电脑甚至笔记本电脑充电。

4. The first 25 stations will be distributed around the city's 5 boroughs, an idea that is sure to spread to other cities in the near future, so watch out for a mobile charging station near you soon.

最先的 25 站将分布在该市的 5 个区,一个想法是在不久的将来蔓延到其他城市,所以移动充电站很快就会在你附近出现。

Unit 2

A. Text

Introduction of Endurance's New Products

Endurance's line of modern, induction-based wind turbines brings efficient, reliable, safe and quiet renewable energy to homeowners, businesses and institutions across Europe, North America and an expanding global market.

Endurance owns the highest producing 50kW turbine technology and also offers a 225kW turbine technology, which it licenses from Norwin in its targeted geographies.

Our E-Series 50kW turbine is offered with the following tower height options: 80 ft (30m), 120 ft (36m) and 140 ft (42m).

The Endurance E-3120 50kW wind turbine (Figure 6-4) is designed to produce renewable energy efficiently, reliably, safely, and quietly. This turbine is ideal for larger farms, schools, hospitals, and commercial/industrial sites, and will produce 100,000~250,000 kWh per year in appropriate winds.

The X-29 225kW wind turbine (Figure 6-5) is designed to produce renewable energy efficiently, reliably, safely, and quietly. This larger mid-size turbine provides the advantage of economies of scale while still making a suitable fit to rural landscapes. This turbine is ideal for farms, municipalities and communities, and will produce 200~850 MWh per year in appropriate winds.

Embracing design principles that have been instrumental to the growing success of large scale wind farms, Endurance has focused on a number of critical design attributes:

1. Production Efficiency

Endurance's E-Series 50kW product highlights include:

* Large 290m^2 swept area (19.2m DIA) —captures more energy

Figure 6-4　E-3120 50kW turbine　　　　Figure 6-5　X-29 225kW turbine

* Induction generator, no invertors—we have zero electrical conversion loss
* High kWh production and lowest cost per kWh in its class
* Peak capacity output in wind speeds between 5.5 and 7.5m/s

2. Reliability

Engineering excellence and exhaustive testing are the cornerstones of our wind turbine design, production and deployment process. Throughout initial design and subsequent revisions, all of our models are manufactured to ensure our customers can count on their turbines over a 20-year lifespan. We also offer a standard 5-year warranty on parts and labor for all Endurance products. A 10-year warranty is also available on the X-29 225kW wind turbine.

3. Safe Operation

Endurance wind turbines are installed in residential settings, university campuses and hospital parking lots. Safety is our number one priority at Endurance Wind Power.

Safety features include:

The ERIC (Endurance Remote Interface Center) system allows Endurance turbine owners to remotely monitor their turbine's performance via a website from anywhere in the world. ERIC enables users to monitor their turbine's operational status, live energy production, power output, wind speed, and offset carbon emissions while operating securely on a VPN network.

4. Quiet Operation

Quiet operation is a must for modern distributed wind turbines. Endurance has focused on minimizing noise output throughout the operating range of our turbines. Even at higher wind speeds, the S, G and E series wind turbines are so quiet that they will not drown out a background conversation between two people.

5. Clean Aesthetics

Whether Endurance wind turbines are being installed in residential, rural or business settings, the visual impact of our turbines is important to our customers. Clean lines and smooth transitions from blades to nacelle and tower ensure that Endurance wind turbines are pleasing to the eye in any landscape.

New Words and Expressions

induction-based [in'dʌkʃnbeisd]	adj. 感应的
municipality [mjuːnisi'pæləti]	n. 市，自治市
instrumental [ˌinstru'mentl]	adj. 有帮助的，起作用的
reliability [riˌlaiə'biləti]	n. 可靠性
cornerstone ['kɔːnəstəʊn]	n. 基石
lifespan ['laifspæn]	n. 使用期，寿命
warranty ['wɒrənti]	n. 保修
deployment process	部署过程
clean aesthetics	清洁美学

Technical Terms

exhaustive testing	穷举测试，详尽测试
production efficiency	生产效率
induction generator	感应发电机
electrical conversion loss	电气转换损耗
peak capacity	峰值容量

Notes

1. Endurance 英国公司名，主要的业务是风电开发，风机生产。

2. Endurance's line of modern, induction-based wind turbines brings efficient, reliable, safe and quiet renewable energy to homeowners, businesses and institutions across Europe, North America and an expanding global market.

Endurance 现代性的感应风力涡轮机生产线为整个欧洲、北美及不断扩大的全球市场的房主、企业和机构带来了高效、可靠、安全和安静的可再生能源。

3. The ERIC (Endurance Remote Interface Center) system allows Endurance turbine owners to remotely monitor their turbine's performance via a website from anywhere in the world.

Endurance 远程接口中心系统允许 Endurance 涡轮机主从世界各地通过网站远程监控他们的涡轮机性能。

4. Quiet operation is a must for modern distributed wind turbines. Endurance has focused on minimizing noise output throughout the operating range of our turbines.

静音操作是现代分布式风力涡轮机的一个必备要求。Endurance 已专注于在涡轮机的操作范围内减少噪声输出。

5. Clean lines and smooth transitions from blades to nacelle and tower ensure that Endurance wind turbines are pleasing to the eye in any landscape.

干净的线条以及从叶片到机舱、塔的平稳过渡，确保 Endurance 的风力涡轮机从各个视觉都给你的眼睛带来愉悦。

Exercises

1. Put the following phrases into English：
① 峰值容量　　② 寿命　　③ 转换损耗
④ 生产效率　　⑤ 机舱　　⑥ 可靠性

2. Decide whether the following statements are true or false：
① Endurance X-29 225kW turbine is offered with the following tower height options：80ft（30m），120ft（36m）and 140ft（42m）.
② Endurance offers a standard 10-year warranty on parts and labor for all products.

3. Translate the following sentences：
① Throughout initial design and subsequent revisions, all of our models are manufactured to ensure our customers can count on their turbines over a 20-year lifespan.
② ERIC enables users to monitor their turbine's operational status, live energy production, power output, wind speed, and offset carbon emissions while operating securely on a VPN network.
③ Even at higher wind speeds, the S, G and E series wind turbines are so quiet that they will not drown out a background conversation between two people.

B. Reading

Hybrid Towers Prevail!

Some of today's wind turbine towers project more than 150 metres into the sky. Above all this is due to the sharp increase in plant performance. Less than 100 metres of rotor diameter is only enough to keep multi-megawatt generators moving at ideal locations. The trend is toward 115 metres and higher (Figure 6-6). Tower height should at least match this diameter, with a measure of one and a half even better. What holds true in any case is the higher, the better. Greater heights mean less turbulence caused by soil roughness and also increasing wind velocities.

This is shown particularly well by the high resolution simulations of the Baden-Württemberg Wing Atlas. Between 100 and 140 metres hub height wind velocities increase by an annual average of 0.2 to 0.3 metres per second. This doubles the number of locations that can be operated economical, particularly since higher towers also increase the feasibility of forest sites. With these figures it also becomes clear that the additional costs

Figure 6-6   Erection of a 128-metre hybrid tower in Clauen near Hildesheim

for greater height are quickly amortized.

Tower construction also changes with the respective heights. In situ concrete towers that are poured on site in vertically rising formwork are becoming less important—just as latticed mast towers. Although both have their advantages in terms of delivery, they are at a disadvantage with their high production and assembly costs. Latticed masts were able to compensate this disadvantage for a time because of high steel prices. Offering comparable rigidity they can be realized with half as much steel as steel tube towers. At present, however, steel prices are dropping once again. On the other hand domestic labour costs remain high. And, in addition, there are problems of acceptance. Lattice towers are rejected by many local residents presumably because they are reminiscent of high voltage masts. Moreover, they require more space; for example, there are 22 metres between the four platform legs in the case of a 160-metre lattice tower that bears a Fuhrländer turbine in Laasow near Cottbus.

Beyond the 100 metre mark even conventional steel tube towers are limited with regard to vibration. Here the industry increasingly relies on a combination of concrete and steel. For the E70 and E80, Enercon offers pure steel towers up to 85 and 78 metres in height, respectively. "Anything higher is implemented with hybrid tower," explains Ruth Brandschock, head of the Enercon office in Berlin. Hybrid towers (Figure 6-7) have proven to be much more resistant to vibration. Approximately five sixths of their design consists of concrete parts, each of which has a section of steel tubing on top. As a rule the necessary concrete segments are delivered.

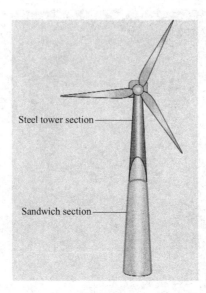

Figure 6-7　A hybrid tower made of steel and concrete

For the lower tower, Enercon puts together three concrete segments of 120 degrees each. Half-shells are then used for the upper parts where the tower diameter tapers off. Other suppliers use tower tubes made of eight concrete components because of simpler delivery. Per section they thus connect four flat concrete walls with four rounded off 90-degree corner elements. They are then strutted from the inside with steel cables before the next eight elements are mounted. Only the top section contains a piece of steel tube over approximately twenty metres-which is required in any case for screw connection of the nacelle.

Pure steel towers have begun to catch up as a result of improve steel alloys. The firmer steel resists vibration and also allows for thinner walls—and thus the use of less material. However, this development has its limits. In extreme cases the structural design of the tower does not allow for any other tolerances in order to attach components such as, for example, ladders on the inside.

New Words and Expressions

project [prə'dʒekt]	v.	伸出，突出
turbulence ['tə:bjələns]	n.	骚动，湍流，动荡
resolution [ˌrezə'lu:ʃn]	n.	分辨率，决心
simulation [ˌsimju'leiʃn]	n.	模拟
feasibility [ˌfi:zə'biləti]	n.	可行性
amortize [ə'mɔ:taiz]	v.	分期偿还（债务）
compensate ['kɒmpenseit]	v.	补偿
rigidity [ri'dʒidəti]	n.	刚度

reminiscent [ˌremiˈnisnt]　　　　　　*adj.* 让人想起的

wind velocity	风速
situ concrete tower	现浇混凝土塔
latticed mast tower	格子桅塔
resistant to vibration	耐振动

1. hybrid tower 混合塔，由钢和混凝土构成，一般塔的底部由混凝土构成，顶部由钢构成。

2. Baden-Württemberg 巴登-符腾堡州，简称巴符州，是德国西南部的一个联邦州。

3. Fuhrländer 德国富兰德公司，一个风机公司。

4. Laasow 德国东部村庄拉斯诺。

5. Cottbus 德国东部的一座城市科特布斯。

6. Enercon 一个德国公司，是全球风电行业的领军企业。

7. Less than 100 metres of rotor diameter is only enough to keep multi-megawatt generators moving at ideal locations.

小于100米的转子直径只够维持几兆瓦的发电机在理想的位置转动。

8. Greater heights mean less turbulence caused by soil roughness and also increasing wind velocities.

更高的高度意味着更少的由土质粗糙度引起的湍流，同时也增加了风速。

9. Although both have their advantages in terms of delivery, they are at a disadvantage with their high production and assembly costs.

虽然两者在传送方面各有优势，但它们在高的生产率和组装成本上处于劣势。

10. However, this development has its limits. In extreme cases the structural design of the tower does not allow for any other tolerances in order to attach components such as, for example, ladders on the inside.

然而，这方面的发展有其自身的局限性。在极端的情况下，塔的结构设计不允许为了附加组件有任何其他偏差，例如，在里面的梯子。

Unit 3

A. Text

Wind-Solar Hybrid Power Station

Scenery complementary power generation system suitable for supplying the coastal islands, lakes, fishing family lighting, color TV, DVD, computer and electric apparatus, the day the sun light and wind, or although cloudy and windy, the system will be solar and wind energy into electric energy on one hand by the inverter outputs AC for family use, hand to charge the battery electrical energy can be stored. The evening by battery power inverter is converted to alternating current for family use, such as the wind at night can continue to provide electric energy. In case of cloudy and windless days, stored in the electric energy of the battery still can maintain the normal power supply 8~12 hours.

Scenery complementary power generation system can maximize the use of natural solar and wind energy, not only clean and environmental protection and is free of charge. Scenery complementary power generation system than the pure solar power system low cost, guarantee the power supply time is long, is a new energy family in a relatively ideal.

Scenery generating system (Figure 6-8) consists of solar photovoltaic battery plate, wind generator, battery charge and discharge inverse integral machine, the solar energy and wind power generator to the battery charge and discharge of the battery by CPU for automatic control, preventing reverse connection, the over-voltage and over-current and undervoltage protection, the wind turbine generator brake protection.

Figure 6-8　A wind-solar hybrid power station

New Words and Expressions

coastal ['kəʊstl]　　　　　　　　　　adj. 沿海的
maintain [meɪn'teɪn]　　　　　　　　v. 保持
over-voltage [ˌəʊvə'vəʊltɪdʒ]　　　　adj. 过压
over-current [ˌəʊvə'kʌrənt]　　　　　adj. 过流

electric apparatus 电器设备
environmental protection 环境保护

Technical Terms

scenery complementary 风光互补
battery plate 电池板
undervoltage protection 欠压保护

Notes

1. Scenery complementary power generation system suitable for supplying the coastal islands, lakes, fishing family lighting, color TV, DVD, computer and electric apparatus, the day the sun light and wind, or although cloudy and windy, the system will be solar and wind energy into electric energy on one hand by the inverter outputs AC for family use, hand to charge the battery electrical energy can be stored.

风光互补发电系统适用于供给沿海岛屿、湖泊、渔夫家庭照明、彩色电视、DVD、计算机和其他电器。在白天有光照和风，甚或是多云和多风时，该系统将太阳能和风能转化为电能，一方面通过逆变器输出交流电供家庭使用，另一方面给电池充电存储电能。

2. Scenery complementary power generation system than the pure solar power system low cost, guarantee the power supply time is long, is a new energy family in a relatively ideal.

风光互补发电系统比纯太阳能发电系统成本低，保证供电时间长，是一个较为理想的新能源家族。

3. Scenery generating system consists of solar photovoltaic battery plate, wind generator, battery charge and discharge inverse integral machine, the solar energy and wind power generator to the battery charge and discharge of the battery by CPU for automatic control, preventing reverse connection, the over-voltage and over-current and undervoltage protection, the wind turbine generator brake protection.

风光互补发电系统由太阳能光伏电池板、风力发电机、电池充电和放电逆变一体机组成，太阳能和风力发电机对电池充电和放电由 CPU 自动控制，用于防反接、过压过流、欠压保护，风机制动器保护。

Exercises

1. Put the following phrases into English:
① 风光互补　　② 电池板　　③ 欠压保护
④ 过流保护　　⑤ 电器设备　　⑥ 保持

2. Decide whether the following statements are true or false:

① Scenery complementary power generation system is suitable for supplying all kinds of families.

② The day the sun light and wind, or although cloudy and windy, the system will be solar and wind energy into electric energy by the inverter outputs AC for family use, but not to charge the battery.

③ The solar energy and wind power generator to the battery charge and discharge of the battery is controlled by CPU.

3. Translate the following sentences:

① The evening by battery power inverter is converted to alternating current for family use, such as the wind at night can continue to provide electric energy.

② Scenery complementary power generation system can maximize the use of natural solar and wind energy, not only clean and environmental protection and is free of charge.

③ Scenery complementary power generation system than the pure solar power system low cost, guarantee the power supply time is long, is a new energy family in a relatively ideal.

B. Reading

Demonstration Project Application of Scenery Complementary

1. Application background

Haitang Bay scenery charming is located in the northeast coast of Sanya City, Hainan Province, and 28 kilometers away from Sanya City, to the south adjacent to Yalong Bay National Resort District. In the early establishment of the province's overall planning of urban development in Sanya, Haitang Bay was classified as a separate group, with a total area of 100 square kilometers planning. Its orientation is mainly to the development of ecological city group research, international exchanges, tourism and sightseeing tropical garden. Now the Haitang Bay area has been identified as "national coastal" theme concept. The development of Haitang Bay should be based on the protection of ecological resources, resource utilization. Haitang Bay based on the formation of public tourism resort, has a unique landscape, new tourism products and high-end coastal tourism resort.

Complementary scenery, as a branch of the new energy industry power supply technology, with its flexible combination, which can leave the network or embedded power, caused the attention of Haitang Bay government. Because of good condition in Haitang Bay, strong public awareness of saving energy, we sincerely advice in Haitang Bay to carry out a comprehensive scenery complementary series of demonstration project application, create a new situation in the work of energy-saving emission reduction, lay a good foundation for the "Twelve five" and even more long-term development, accelerate transformation of the mode of economic development, realize scientific development, promote the process of building a well-off society and make new contributions.

2. Sanya area wind, light and other natural conditions

Sanya is a tropical marine monsoon climate, the annual average temperature of

25.7℃, the average annual rainfall of 1347.5 mm, and annual sunny day more than three hundred days. Sunny, long summer without winter, Sanya is well-known all over the world as a winter holiday resort, exporting to the world its sunshine and air. The average annual total solar radiation is 131600 kcal/square centimeter, annual sunshine 2000 to 2750 hours, the average annual solar scattering of radiation 2.02kW · h/(m² · d), average annual solar radiation exposure 3.91kW · h/(m² · d), and the optimal average annual solar radiation amount 4.79kW · h/(m² · d). The annual average wind speed is 2.2m/s, perennial in the winter wind turns stronger, in November and December the average wind speed is 2.9m/s, and the average speed of wind in August is minimum 2.1m/s. In the past 50 years the maximum wind speed is 48m/s. Sanya has monsoon climate characteristics, obvious northeast monsoon in winter and southwest monsoon in summer.

From the meteorological data in the past, Sanya city scenery resources are very rich, provide good working conditions for solar and wind power generators. In addition, the wind resources in Sanya city in winter stronger than in summer, the solar energy resources in summer richer than winter, it provides good working conditions for wind-light complementary system, so the stability and reliability of the system are improved greatly.

3. Project overview

Haitang Bay area has a good wind, light and natural conditions, the community awareness on energy conservation is high and the new energy applications have a good foundation. The strong financial resources vigorously promote the use of clean energy, environmental protection and sustainable development of economy and society. The scenery complementary demonstration project aims (Figure 6-9) to create a good atmosphere of low carbon economic development, build a new energy demonstration window. The current implementation of the scenery complementary demonstration project concludes street lamp, landscape lamp, outdoor advertising, light box, bus shelter, communication base

Figure 6-9　Kunming lake road scenery complementary road lighting project

station, road monitoring, toilet and photovoltaic roof power field. Nearly hundreds of media reported, as the first scenery complementary large-scale application, the exemplary and leading role of "Haitang Bay mode" is very positive.

4. Benefit analysis

As an example, using a road scenery complementary lamp in 10 years, to replace the traditional 250W lamp, you can save electricity of 10768kW·h, equivalent to save 4308kg standard coal, to reduce emissions of 2929kg carbon dust, 10736kg CO_2, and 323kg SO_2. According to the current price, 0.6 yuan/kW·h, the government can save 6461 yuan in 10 years. The economic benefits, social benefits, and environmental benefits are obvious, so the scenery complementary application has a very great prospect.

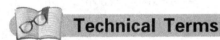

New Words and Expressions

high-end [haiend]	adj. 高端的
rainfall ['reinfɔːl]	n. 降雨
perennial [pəreniəl]	adj. 终年的，长久的
exemplary [iɡˈzempləri]	adj. 典型的，示范的
vigorously [ˈviɡərəsli]	adv. 精神旺盛地，活泼地，大力
tourism and sightseeing tropical garden	旅游观光的热带花园
theme concept	主题概念
well-off society	小康社会

Technical Terms

tropical marine monsoon climate	热带海洋性季风气候
meteorological data	气象数据

Notes

1. Haitang Bay scenery charming is located in the northeast coast of Sanya City, Hainan Province, and 28 kilometers away from Sanya City, to the south adjacent to Yalong Bay National Resort District.

海棠湾风光迷人，位于海南省东北海岸的三亚市，距三亚市区28公里，南与亚龙湾国家旅游度假区相邻。

2. Now the Haitang Bay area has been identified as "national coastal" theme concept. The development of Haitang Bay should be based on the protection of ecological resources, resource utilization. Haitang Bay based on the formation of public tourism resort, has a unique landscape, new tourism products and has become high-end coastal tourism resort.

现在，海棠湾地区已被确定为"国家海岸"的主题概念，海棠湾的发展当以生态资源保护、资源利用、环境优美为基础。海棠湾基于公共旅游度假区形式为基础，具有独特的景观、新的旅游产品，并成为高端滨海旅游度假区。

3. The average annual total solar radiation is 131600 kcal / square centimeter, annual sunshine 2000 to 2750 hours, the average annual solar scattering of radiation 2.02kW·h/(m² · d), average annual solar radiation exposure 3.91kW·h/(m² · d), and the optimal average annual solar radiation amount 4.79kW·h/(m² · d).

年平均太阳总辐射为131600千卡/平方厘米，年日照时数2000～2750小时，年平均太阳辐射是2.02千瓦时/(平方米·天)，年平均太阳辐射直射3.91千瓦时/(平方米·天)，年平均太阳辐射最佳达4.79千瓦时/(平方米·天)。

4. In addition, the wind resources in Sanya city in winter stronger than in summer, the solar energy resources in summer richer than winter, it provides good working conditions for wind-light complementary system, so the stability and reliability of the system are improved greatly.

此外，风能资源在三亚市冬季优于夏季，太阳能资源在夏季优于冬季，这为风光互补系统提供良好的工作条件，从而大大提高了系统的稳定性和可靠性。

Unit 4

A. Text

WD Series Biomass Burners

WD series biomass burner (Figure 6-10), designed and manufactured by our company, is the main equipment that uses biomass for energy conversion. It is the best choice of the energy saving and upgrading production of coal stove, electric stove, oil furnace and gas furnace.

Figure 6-10　WD series biomass burner

Product features:

① Complete combustion and high efficiency: Boiling gasification combustion Gache line with the wind swirling design makes complete combustion burner, the combustion efficiency of up to 95%.

② Safe and stable combustion: Equipment in positive pressure mode operation, do not occur the phenomenon of backfire and fire off.

③ Heat load adjustment range: Burner heat load at rated load 30%~120% range quickly adjust, start fast and responsive.

④ Wide raw material adaptability: All kinds of biomass raw material, which moisture less than 30% and size less than 30mm can be used in this equipment, such as corn stalks, rick husks, peanuts shells, corn cobs, sawdust, wood shavings, paper scrap etc.

⑤ None-pollution and obvious environment benefits: Use renewable biomass as fuel in order to achieve a sustainable use of energy. Adapt low temperature staged combustion technique, which makes the emission of NO_x, SO_2 and dust very low.

⑥ No waste emission such as tar and wastewater: Adopt high temperature gas directly combustion technology, tar and others will directly burn in the form of gas, which can solve the technical problem of high tar emission from biomass gasification, avoid the water secondary contamination from washing tar.

⑦ Simple operation and easy maintenance: Automatic feeding and wind ash, simple operation, small workload, only need a single person on duty.

⑧ High heating temperature: This technology uses three times with the wind, to ensure the flow of the jet region normally under the furnace pressure in 5000-7000 Pa.

⑨ Wide application of the equipment: WD series burners are used as residential boilers, small electric station boilers, furnace boilers or other heating devices.

⑩ Low investment and low operation costs: WD series biomass burners have reasonable design structure. Low-cost when transfer for other furnace use, and the working costs of heating is 30%~40% lower than coal-fire boiler and 50%~70% lower than oil-fired boiler.

New Words and Expressions

responsive [ri'spɒnsiv]	adj.	响应的
adaptability [ədæptə'biləti]	n.	适应性
moisture ['mɔistʃə(r)]	n.	水分
tar [tɑː(r)]	n.	焦油
contamination [kənˌtæmi'neiʃən]	n.	污染
sawdust ['sɔːdʌst]	n.	木屑
corn stalk		玉米秸秆
rick husk		里克稻壳
peanuts shell		花生壳
corn cob		玉米棒

wood shaving	刨花
paper scrap	纸屑
furnace boiler	炉膛锅炉

Technical Terms

biomass burner	生物质燃烧器
coal stove	煤炉
electric stove	电炉
oil furnace	燃油炉
gas furnace	煤气炉

Notes

1. WD series biomass burner, designed and manufactured by our company, is the main equipment that uses biomass for energy conversion.

由我们公司设计制造的 WD 系列生物质燃烧器，是使用生物质转换能量的主要设备。

2. Boiling gasification combustion Gache line with the wind swirling design makes complete combustion burner, the combustion efficiency of up to 95%.

沸腾风旋流燃烧器的设计是完全气化燃烧加切线，燃烧效率高达 95%。

3. All kinds of biomass raw material, which moisture less than 30% and size less than 30mm can be used in this equipment, such as corn stalks, rick husks, peanuts shells, corn cobs, sawdust, wood shavings, paper scrap etc.

各种水分比例小于 30% 和尺寸不到 30mm 的生物质原料可以使用这种设备，如玉米秸秆、稻壳、花生壳、玉米棒子、木屑、刨花、纸屑等。

4. WD series burners are used as residential boilers, small electric station boilers, furnace boilers or other heating devices.

WD 系列燃烧器作为住宅锅炉、电站小锅炉、普通锅炉或其他加热装置使用。

Exercises

1. Put the following phrases into English:
   ① 生物质燃烧器　② 污染　③ 电炉
   ④ 气化　⑤ 燃烧　⑥ 响应

2. Decide whether the following statements are true or false:
   ① WD series burners have no requirement on the size or the humidity of materials.
   ② WD series burners don't waste emission such as tar and wastewater.
   ③ WD series burner is a kind of low investment but high operation costs.

3. Translate the following sentences:

① Use renewable biomass as fuel so that achieve a sustainable use of energy. Adapt low temperature staged combustion technique, which makes the emission of NO_x, SO_2 and dust is very low.

② Automatic feeding and wind ash, simple operation, small workload, only need a single person on duty.

③ Low-cost when transfer for other furnace use, and the working costs of heating is 30%～40% lower than coal-fire boiler and 50%～70% lower than oil-fired boiler.

B. Reading

What Chevron Is Doing for Geothermal Energy?

Geothermal energy is created by the heat of the earth. It generates reliable power and emits almost no greenhouse gases.

This is how it works (Figure 6-11): When groundwater seeps below the earth's surface near a dormant volcano, the water is heated by reservoirs of molten rock, usually at depths of up to 9,800 feet (3,000 m). Wells similar to those used to produce crude oil and natural gas are drilled to recover the water. Once captured, steam and hot water are separated. The steam is cleaned and sent to the power plant. The separated water is returned to the reservoir, where it helps to regenerate the steam source.

Figure 6-11 Chevron's geothermal operations at the Salak Field in Indonesia produce steam to generate reliable power with almost no greenhouse emissions

Very few places provide the special conditions needed to generate geothermal energy. At these locations, deep fractures in the earth's crust allow the molten rock to surge close enough to the surface to heat water underground.

What Are the Benefits?

In addition to providing clean, renewable power, geothermal energy has significant environmental advantages. Geothermal emissions contain few chemical pollutants and little waste—they consist mostly of water, which is reinjected into the ground.

Geothermal energy is a reliable source of power that can reduce the need for imported fuels for power generation. It's also renewable because it is based on a practically limitless resource—natural heat within the earth.

The electricity produced by our geothermal power operations is sold to local power grids, providing clean energy to fuel the growth of some of the world's most rapidly expanding economies.

What Chevron Is Doing?

Chevron is one of the world's leading producers of geothermal energy.

Chevron began geothermal operations during the 1960s by pioneering the development of the Geysers, north of San Francisco, California. In the 1970s, two discoveries in the Philippines led to the development of the Tiwi and Makiling-Banahaw (Mak-Ban) geothermal projects on Luzon. We discovered the Salak and Darajat fields on Java in Indonesia in the 1980s and began commercial production in the 1990s.

Chevron's geothermal interests in Indonesia and the Philippines produce enough renewable geothermal energy to supply millions of people in those countries.

Chevron operates two geothermal projects in Indonesia, Darajat and Salak, which have a combined operating capacity of 636 megawatts.

Chevron also has a 40 percent interest in the Philippine Geothermal Production Company, the operator of the Tiwi geothermal facility in Albay Province and the Mak-Ban geothermal facility in Laguna and Batangas provinces. These fields provide steam to the third-party Tiwi and Mak-Ban geothermal power plants in southern Luzon, which have a combined generating capacity of 637 megawatts.

We are assessing prospects in both countries that could lead to more geothermal energy production.

Geothermal resources represent significant untapped energy. As Chevron continues to pursue geothermal opportunities, we are at the forefront of bringing this clean, renewable energy to our communities.

New Words and Expressions

seep [si:p]	v.	渗透，渗出
reinject [ˌri:in'dʒekt]	v.	重新注入
untapped [ˌʌn'tæpt]	adj.	未开发的
forefront ['fɔ:frʌnt]	n.	前沿
dormant volcano		休眠火山
reservoir of molten rock		融化的岩石层

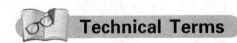 Technical Terms

greenhouse gas　　　　　　　　　　　　二氧化碳、甲烷等导致温室效应的气体

 Notes

1. Chevron 美国第二大石油公司——雪佛龙股份有限公司，是世界最大的全球能源公司之一。

2. When groundwater seeps below the earth's surface near a dormant volcano, the water is heated by reservoirs of molten rock, usually at depths of up to 9,800 feet (3,000m).
当地下水渗漏到休眠火山附近的地表面之下，水被熔化的岩石层加热，这通常在9800英尺（3000米）左右的深度。

3. In addition to providing clean, renewable power, geothermal energy has significant environmental advantages. Geothermal emissions contain few chemical pollutants and little waste—they consist mostly of water, which is reinjected into the ground.
除了提供清洁、可再生的能源，地热能具有重要的环境优势。地热排放含有极少化学污染物，浪费少，因为它们的主要成分是水，水会被再注入地内。

4. Chevron also has a 40 percent interest in the Philippine Geothermal Production Company, the operator of the Tiwi geothermal facility in Albay Province and the Mak-Ban geothermal facility in Laguna and Batangas provinces.
雪佛龙还拥在菲律宾的地热出品公司百分之四十的股权，是阿尔拜省提维地热设施和拉古纳和八打雁省麦办地热设施的经营者。

Part Ⅶ New Technology

Unit 1

A. Text

The Demise of Solar Silicon Crystals?

There's an ongoing debate over the "best" crystals for solar panels—mono-or polycrystalline. You can read about the difference here. Basically, it's a decision of performance vs. cost. SunPower, the massive US manufacturer, believes in performance, the best performance, and that customers will pay more for it. Most of the Chinese manufacturers disagree, and put out low-cost competitive products which don't produce quite the same amount of electricity per panel.

But what if it's the wrong debate?

It's the 1830's in the Russian Ural Mountains about 500 miles East of Moscow (Figure 7-1). A new mineral (fancy word for a shiny rock) is discovered by a German mineralogist called Gustav Rose. He names it perovskite (Figure 7-2), after a Russian mineralogist, and it's a kind of shiny and usually gray crystalline structure. But no one can figure out a use for it. As the years passed, and since it looks kind of boring and there's lots of it all over the world, no particular value was placed on it.

Figure 7-1 The Russian Ural Mountains about 500 miles East of Moscow

Zip forward to 2009, around 17 decades later, some bright spark decided to try to make solar photo-voltaic cells from it. Bingo!

Although there were some initial challenges with efficiency, the big news is that a perovskite panel capturing the same light energy as a silicon panel is less than 1% of the

Figure 7-2 Perovskite

thickness of the silicon product. This has huge implications for reducing manufacturing and shipping costs.

Current silicon based photo-voltaic cells get an efficiency rating—in the lab—of 21% at the maximum, and more typically in the 13% to 18% range. Current prototypes for the perovskite based cells are delivering 15% already, with the potential for 20% to even as high as 25% in the near future. This is unprecedented, and could turn the silicon-based solar world on its head.

German-born Michael Gratzel (Figure 7-3) is a professor at the elite Swiss Federal Institute of Technology. This guy is a bright cookie, with more publications and awards than you can count, and he's at the forefront of this perovskite research, so we can expect to see more breaking news about perovskite soon.

Figure 7-3 Michael Gratzel

New Words and Expressions

ongoing ['ɒngəʊiŋ]   *adj.* 正在进行的

performance [pəˈfɔːməns]   *n.* 性能

mineralogist [ˌminəˈrælədʒist]　　　　n. 矿物学家
deliver [diˈlivə(r)]　　　　　　　　　v. 发表，递送，交付，使分娩
potential [pəˈtenʃl]　　　　　　　　　adj. 潜在的
unprecedente [ˌʌnpriˈsiːdənt]　　　　adj. 前所未有的
forefront Zip forward to 2009　　　　时间快进到2009年

Technical Terms

mono- or poly-crystalline　　　　　　单晶或者多晶
efficiency rating　　　　　　　　　　效率评价，效率值

Notes

1. SunPower 世界最强大的太阳能公司之一，集开发、设计、生产和销售高效、高可靠性太阳能电池片、组件和系统为一体的美国光伏公司。

2. Perovskite 钙钛矿，这类化合物具有稳定的晶体结构、独特的电磁性能以及很高的氧化还原、氢解、异构化、电催化等活性，作为一种新型的功能材料，在环境保护和工业催化等领域具有很大的开发潜力。

3. There's an ongoing debate over the "best" crystals for solar panels—mono- or poly-crystalline.
单晶或者多晶，哪个才是最好的太阳能电池板材料？这是个正在辩论的问题。

4. Most of the Chinese manufacturers disagree, and put out low-cost competitive products which don't produce quite the same amount of electricity per panel.
大多数中国制造商不同意这个观点，他们生产出低成本的竞争产品，这种产品每块电池板产生的电量也相对较少。

5. As the years passed, and since it looks kind of boring and there's lots of it all over the world, no particular value was placed on it.
随着岁月流逝，由于它看起来有些无趣，而且全世界到处都是，所以并没有体现出特别的价值。

6. Although there were some initial challenges with efficiency, the big news is that a perovskite panel capturing the same light energy as a silicon panel is less than 1% of the thickness of the silicon product. This has huge implications for reducing manufacturing and shipping costs.
虽然有一些初始的效率上的挑战，但是一个很大的新闻是这种钙钛矿电池板在获得和一块硅电池板一样多光能的情况下，厚度却是硅产品的1%。这对降低生产和运输成本有着巨大的影响。

7. Current prototypes for the perovskite based cells are delivering 15% already, with the potential for 20% to even as high as 25% in the near future. This is unprecedented, and could turn the silicon-based solar world on its head.

目前钙钛矿电池转换效率已经达到15%，在不久的将来可能达到20%甚至25%。这是前所未有的，它能把基于硅的太阳能世界推向顶峰。

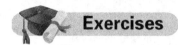

Exercises

1. Put the following phrases into English：

① 硅　　　② 矿石　　　③ 性能
④ 原型　　⑤ 单晶硅　　⑥ 传送

2. Decide whether the following statements are true or false：

① For a long time in the past, the value of perovskite hadn't been found.

② Most of the Chinese manufacturers believe in the best performance, and that customers will pay more for it.

③ Current prototypes for the perovskite based cells get the more efficiency rating than current silicon based photo-voltaic cells.

3. Translate the following sentences：

① SunPower, the massive US manufacturer, believes in performance, the best performance, and that customers will pay more for it.

② Current silicon based photo-voltaic cells get an efficiency rating—in the lab—of 21% at the maximum, and more typically in the 13% to 18% range.

③ This guy is a bright cookie, with more publications and awards than you can count, and he's at the forefront of this perovskite research, so we can expect to see more breaking news about perovskite soon.

B. Reading

Solar Mobile Device Chargers—Welcome to the 21st Century!

There's a scene in the original Lethal Weapon movie where Danny Glover's character (Figure 7-4) is outside talking with a psychiatrist back at the police precinct. He's on talking on a cell phone, and not only is it huge, but also it's linked by a cable to a battery the size of a lunch box and weighing several pounds. It was state of the art in its day, the mid to late 80's.

Fast forward almost 3 decades and the cell phone technology (which most of us take for granted) is truly mind-blowing. And along with the electronic developments have come some remarkable advances in battery technology to keep our devices small and light, while running for hours. But no matter how efficient the batteries get, we always want more apps on brighter screens with better sound, so the batteries invariably need charging "on the go".

Enter the world of solar powered battery charges.

These seriously handy solar gadgets range from the simple & low cost to the technically superior and more costly. We'll look at a couple of examples here.

Figure 7-4 Danny Glover

First up is the *Opteka BP-SC*4000 (Figure 7-5) —it's a thin solar powered backup battery and charger combined, and can be used to charge cell phones and other mobile devices. It packs a weighty 4Ah battery, offers 10 different charging connectors plus a USB port, and will auto-shut-off when charging of your device is complete. The unit can be charged by its USB port, or via the handy built-in solar panel. At around $25, this is a great option for people on the go without access to a charger, who need an occasional extra charge on their cell phone to get them through the day.

Figure 7-5 Opteka BP-SC4000

Higher up the solar charger food chain is the Joos Orange (Figure 7-6) by Solar Joos, coming in at around $150. This charger packs a powerful punch, and claims to capture 20 times more solar energy than comparable chargers, and provide a couple of hours talk time

Figure 7-6 Joos Orange

on your phone for each hour it spends charging in the sun. As a backup power source it can be charged with a USB power adapter. And if you like being at the beach or the pool, don't worry—the Orange keeps charging under water! Only question we have is, why is it gray colored?

New Words and Expressions

psychiatrist [saiˈkaiətrist]	n. 精神科医生
mind-blowing [ˈmaindˌbləʊiŋ]	adj. 令人兴奋的
invariably [inˈveəriəbli]	adv. 总是；不变地
occasional [əˈkeiʒənl]	adj. 偶尔的
apps	abbr. appendices 附录，应用程序
police precinct	警察分局，警署
Fast forward almost 3 decades	进 30 年的快速前进
on the go	活跃，忙个不停

Technical Terms

backup power source	备用电源

Notes

1. Danny Glover 丹尼·格洛弗，美国男演员、导演、制片。

2. He's on talking on a cell phone, and not only is it huge, but also it's linked by a cable to a battery the size of a lunch box and weighing several pounds.

他正在通话，所用的手机不仅大，而且由一根电缆和一个饭盒般大小并且有几磅重的电池相连。

3. And along with the electronic developments have come some remarkable advances in battery technology to keep our devices small and light, while running for hours.

随着电子发展，在电池技术方面有了显著的进步，它使我们的设备小而轻，且运行数小时。

4. But no matter how efficient the batteries get, we always want more apps on brighter screens with better sound, so the batteries invariably need charging 'on the go'.

但是不管电池如何有效，我们总是想要在更亮的屏幕上、带有更好听声音的情况下来使用更多的应用程序，所以电池总是需要忙个不停地充电。

5. It packs a weighty 4Ah battery, offers 10 different charging connectors plus a USB port, and will auto-shut-off when charging of your device is complete.

它装有 4 安时电池，提供 10 种不同的充电连接器以及一个 USB 接口，在充电完成时自动关闭。

6. This charger packs a powerful punch, and claims to capture 20 times more solar energy than comparable chargers, and provide a couple of hours talk time on your phone for each hour it spends charging in the sun.

该充电器有很厉害的地方,声称可捕获比一般电池多 20 倍的太阳能,并且在阳光下充一个小时电就能给你的手机提供几小时的通话时间。

Unit 2

A. Text

Wind Power—The Basics

Everyone's seen wind turbines (Figure 7-7)—either in real life or on TV. The basic idea is that wind turns the propeller-like blades, and this induced motion or "kinetic" energy is converted into electrical energy via an alternator. The concept is similar to that of using some of your car engine's energy to charge the car battery using the alternator. With a wind turbine any generated electricity is then used locally or transmitted along power lines to remote locations, typically along the main power grid.

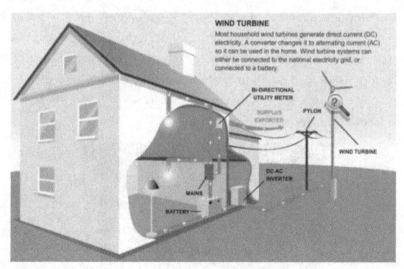

Figure 7-7 Wind turbine

So if the idea is so simple, and wind is available pretty much everywhere, why don't we see more wind turbines? Well, the answer lies primarily in cost and esthetics. To generate enough electricity for an average sized home, you'd need a large turbine (Figure 7-8) generating in the area of 10 kilo-Watts, and costing anywhere from $30,000 to $70,000. In addition, you need land. It's possible that the turbine may need to be up to 80 feet or more in the air to clear trees and buildings, and need guy lines tying it securely—which can extend 60 feet or more out from the main post. Installation is also no easy feat—it's not a D.I.Y. Project—unless you can drive a crane, which is needed to hoist up the tower.

Figure7-8　A large turbine for an average sized home

Which means wind power is not typically suited to suburban or urban areas, but more likely a fit for rural locations.

Plus, you have huge blades on a big tower in your back garden.

So there's a lot to consider. However, the upside is potentially big—free electricity powered by the wind, and once your setup is paid, it's all bonus money for the life of the turbine, with minimal overhead.

This technology is certainly simple in concept, but very advanced in execution, with the efficiency of energy conversion in a constantly improving field of endeavor. Also, as with solar power solutions, wind power is not "all or nothing"—you can start with smaller roof-mounted systems to offset small portions of your electric bill, or to charge battery systems for backup power. You'll find more articles on this site about the technical aspects of wind power, large-scale installations with seriously impressive power delivery, and even wind farms (Figure 7-9) in the ocean.

Figure 7-9　Wind farms in the ocean

Your local wind power contractor can best advise you if this is a viable alternative energy solution for you—you can click the link at the top of any page to find an installer.

New Words and Expressions

propeller-like [prəˈpelə(r) laik]　　　　adj. 螺旋桨式的

esthetic [es'θetik]	n. 美学
crane [krein]	n. 吊车,起重机
endeavor [en'devə]	n. 努力
bonus money	奖金

Technical Terms

hoist up	吊起来
power grid	电网
minimal overhead	最小的开销

Notes

1. The basic idea is that wind turns the propeller-like blades, and this induced motion or "kinetic" energy is converted into electrical energy via an alternator.

基本的想法是风转动螺旋桨状叶片,这引起的运动的能量通过一个交流发电机转化为电能。

2. Installation is also no easy feat—it's not a D. I. Y. Project—unless you can drive a crane, which is needed to hoist up the tower. Which means wind power is not typically suited to suburban or urban areas, but more likely a fit for rural locations.

安装也并不容易,它不是一个自己动手的项目,除非你能驱动一架起重机来吊起塔。这意味着风力通常不适合城郊或城市地区,但更适合农村地区。

3. However, the upside is potentially big—free electricity powered by the wind, and once your setup is paid, it's all bonus money for the life of the turbine, with minimal overhead.

然而,好处其实很大:免费的风力发的用电,而且一旦你设置付账,它将是以最小的开销支付了涡轮机整个使用周期。

4. Your local wind power contractor can best advise you if this is a viable alternative energy solution for you—you can click the link at the top of any page to find an installer.

如果这是一个可行的替代能源的解决方案,你们当地的风力发电商可以给你最好的建议;你可以点击任何页面顶部的链接找到一个安装程序。

Exercises

1. Put the following phrases into English:
① 电网   ② 起重机   ③ 开销
④ 奖金   ⑤ 交流发电机   ⑥ 涡轮机

2. Decide whether the following statements are true or false:

① All of generated electricity with a wind turbine is used locally.

② This technology is certainly simple in concept, but very advanced in execution, with the efficiency of energy conversion in a constantly improving field of endeavor.

③ The installation of the wind turbine is easy, and a family can install it completely.

④ Wind power is not typically suited to suburban or urban areas, but more likely a fit for rural locations.

3. Translate the following sentences:

① To generate enough electricity for an average sized home, you'd need a large turbine generating in the area of 10 kilo-Watts, and costing anywhere from $30,000 to $70,000. In addition, you need land.

② This technology is certainly simple in concept, but very advanced in execution, with the efficiency of energy conversion a constantly improving field of endeavor.

B. Reading

Commercial Wind Power—An Introduction

Utility companies, farms, large industrial developments, government sites, military installations—these are the typical settings for large scale wind turbine solutions. With costs ranging from several hundred thousand dollars up to $2 million or more per megawatt of installed turbines, you need to be a big player to get serious about wind power (Figure 7-10).

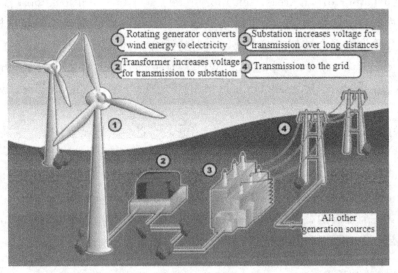

Figure 7-10 Wind power generation system

For example, an average sized farm may commit a half million dollars to a 100kW turbine project, but then reap the massive reward of virtually no energy bill for decades—a huge return on investment for the business.

In addition, and as with solar solutions, there are often local utility companies, State and Federal incentives available for wind power installations. These can hugely affect the return-on-investment math, making the decision easy for any cash-flow-positive business model.

Wind is becoming a more viable option due to the dropping prices of the turbines and their installation. Since 2008 prices have dropped by more than 1/3, creating fast growth in the US and abroad. This has prompted big investments from utility companies looking to supplement current supply and eventually move away from burning fossil fuels to create electricity.

So we have an idea of who may use wind power turbines, but who makes the stuff, and who installs it?

This is a surprisingly robust and growing business, with some great US manufacturers supplying US contractors for installations right here in North America. Aeronautica Windpower (Figure 7-11), out of Plymouth, MA, manufactures mid-scale turbines for businesses across the US. They started up in 2008, and service the niche between large-scale utility turbines and smaller domestic solutions. This means they provide just 3 products—a 225kW, a 500kW and a 750kW machine. Each designed to be quiet, ultra-efficient and long lasting, with minimal maintenance, and with options to finance or lease.

Figure 7-11　Aeronautica logo

Anemometry Specialists, based in Alta, Iowa, is a family owned and operated business running successfully for over a decade. Their dedicated team installs and maintains wind turbine equipment, with over 1700 towers built to date. (Anemometry is the measurement of wind speed and direction). They also provide test equipment to assess your location for suitability for wind turbine installation—an important step before making such a big investment.

 New Words and Expressions

commit [kəˈmit]	v. 做错事，把……托付给，保证，承诺，使……承担义务
virtually [ˈvɜːtʃuəli]	adv. 实际上地
incentive [inˈsentiv]	n. 动机，激励
niche [niːʃ]	n. 有利可图的缺口，商机，合适的位置
range from	范围从
reap the massive reward	收获巨大回报
business mode	商业模式

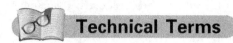

Technical Terms

fossil fuel　　　　　　　　　　　化石燃料
long lasting　　　　　　　　　　 持久的
minimal maintenance　　　　　　最小维修

1. Utility companies, farms, large industrial developments, government sites, military installations—these are the typical settings for large scale wind turbine solutions.

公共事业公司、农场、大工业发展、政府网站以及军事设施,这些都是大型风力发电机组典型的设置应用。

2. For example, an average sized farm may commit a half million dollars to a 100kW turbine project, but then reap the massive reward of virtually no energy bill for decades—a huge return on investment for the business.

例如,一个普通大小的农场可能为了一个100千瓦发电机组项目花费五十万美元,但是获得的巨大收获是数十年都不再需要能源上的花费,这是一个巨大的投资回报。

3. This has prompted big investments from utility companies looking to supplement current supply and eventually move away from burning fossil fuels to create electricity.

这促使公共事业公司想要补充现有的供应进行大的投资,最终摆脱化石燃料燃烧发电。

4. This means they provide just 3 products—a 225kW, a 500kW and a 750kW machine. Each designed to be quiet, ultra-efficient and long lasting, with minimal maintenance, and with options to finance or lease.

这意味着他们只是提供三种产品：225kW、500kW和750kW的机器,每个都静音设计、超高效、持久及最少维护,并可选择购买或租用。

Unit 3

A. Text

Scenery Complementary LED Street Lamp Lighting System

Along with our country city modernization by leaps and bounds, the rapid development of city road lighting, many urban lighting system adopts the traditional lamps and lanterns, which causes huge energy consumption and becomes a heavy burden of local government. According to relevant data shows, the city street lamp lighting power consumption in our country in the proportion of 30%, the annual electricity consumption accounts for the total generating capacity of 4%~5%, and power efficiency in the use of less than 70%, the annual 80 billion yuan of government agency power energy consumption of a city, street lamp lighting part of the energy expenditure to more than 200 million yuan. More than 70% of the existing street lamp use is high pressure sodium lamp, the design life for 24 000 h, but because our country city grid technology is backward, and line voltage fluctuates significantly more than 15% of the rated voltage or so, especially in the wee hours, the reduction of electricity load makes power grid voltage sometimes close to 245V, the street light bulb of the actual service life on average less than 1 year. Along with our country city modernization by leaps and bounds in recent years, the rapid development of city road lighting, the corresponding electricity is increasing by a big margin, and because the power can't store, most of the city's power and time is too concentrated and other factors, the electrical energy efficiency in the use of less than 70%. In general, our country city street lamp lighting mainly there are two big drawbacks:

① all the urban road, the highway, industrial zone, living quarters road, from the evening after light lamps have been light to 6 a.m., this not only shorten the service life of the lighting lamps and lanterns, but also waste a lot of energy, to government created a heavy financial burden;

② the characteristics of the power grid is when the load increases, the voltage is relatively low; reduction of load, the voltage is opposite taller. When the voltage of street lamp, at electricity peak, is low, it becomes darker, and into the middle of the night, the electric load gets down, and the voltage rises with the illumination anomaly bright, even glare appears. It not only causes unnecessary electric energy waste, but also makes the service life of lamps and lanterns being greatly reduced.

To this, some cities began to use high performance LED lamps and lanterns to replace traditional lamps and lanterns, and used the wind energy, solar energy or scenery complementary system for power supply. Of course, the initial investment increased by 50% or so than traditional lighting system, but according to statistics, after three years of use, the scenery complementary LED street lamp lighting system cost is equal to that of traditional lighting system; in the twenty years of service life, the total cost of scenery complementary system is even lower. It not only has the landscape effect, but also protects the environment. In addition, scenery complementary garden lamp, lawn lamp, landscape lamp and so on also improved the ordinary people's quality of life and quality.

 New Words and Expressions

lantern ['læntən]　　　　　　　　　*n.* 灯，灯笼
consumption [kən'sʌmpʃn]　　　　*n.* 消耗，消费

expenditure [ikˈspenditʃə(r)]	n. 支出
margin [ˈmaːdʒin]	n. 边缘，范围，极限，利润，盈余
drawback [ˈdrɔːbæk]	n. 缺点，缺陷
characteristics [ˌkæriktəˈristik]	n. 特征
illumination [iˌluːmiˈneiʃn]	n. 照明
anomaly [əˈnɒməli]	adv. 异常地
city modernization	城市现代化
leaps and bounds	跳跃式发展，突飞猛进
in the wee hours	在凌晨
high performance	高性能
landscape effect	景观效果

Technical Terms

high pressure sodium lamp	高压钠灯

Notes

1. LED lamp LED 灯，最初 LED 用作仪器仪表的指示光源，后来各种光色的 LED 在交通信号灯和大面积显示屏中得到了广泛应用，产生了很好的经济效益和社会效益。近年来，LED 灯开始越来越多地用于普通照明，具有节能、长寿、环保、成本低廉等优点。

2. According to relevant data shows, the city street lamp lighting power consumption in our country in the proportion of 30%, the annual electricity consumption accounts for the total generating capacity of 4%～5%, and power efficiency in the use of less than 70%, the annual 80 billion yuan of government agency power energy consumption of a city, street lamp lighting part of the energy expenditure to more than 200 million yuan.

据有关数据显示，在我国城市路灯照明电力消费的比重为 30%，年消耗电量占总发电量的 4%～5%，使用效率不足 70%，每年政府机构城市能耗费用 800 亿元，路灯照明部分的能量支出超过 2 亿元。

3. All the urban road, the highway, industrial zone, living quarters road, from the evening after light lamps have been light to 6 a.m., this not only shorten the service life of the lighting lamps and lanterns, but also waste a lot of energy, to government created a heavy financial burden.

所有的城市道路、公路、工业区、居住区的道路，从晚上点亮灯开始到早上 6 点，这不仅缩短了照明灯具的使用寿命，而且还浪费了大量的能源，给政府财政造成了沉重的负担。

4. To this, some cities begin to use high performance LED lamps and lanterns to replace traditional lamps and lanterns, and used the wind energy, solar energy or scenery

complementary system for power supply.

对此，一些城市开始使用高性能的 LED 灯具取代传统灯具，利用风能，太阳能或风光互补系统供电。

5. In the twenty years of service life, scenery complementary system called total cost but low, not only has the landscape effect, but also protect the environment.

在二十年的使用寿命里，风光互补系统总成本低，不仅具有景观效果，又保护了环境。

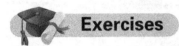

Exercises

1. Put the following phrases into English：
① 路灯　　② 风光互补　　③ 耗电量　　④ 高性能
⑤ 景观效果　⑥ 高压钠灯　　⑦ 支出　　　⑧ 缺点

2. Translating：

① More than 70% of the existing street lamp use is high pressure sodium lamp, the design life for 24 000 h, but because our country city grid technology is backward, cause line voltage fluctuation significantly more than 15% of the rated voltage or so, especially in the wee hours, because electricity load reduce makes power grid voltage sometimes close to 245V, the street light bulb of the actual service life on average less than 1 year.

② the characteristics of the power grid is when the load increases, the voltage is relatively low; Reduction of load, the voltage is opposite taller, street lamp for this kind of gas discharge equipment, in the traffic's a long fall on electricity peak, voltage is low, brightness darker, and into the middle of the night, the electric load down, voltage rises in the illumination anomaly bright, appear even glare, not only cause unnecessary electric energy waste, but also makes the service life of lamps and lanterns is greatly reduced.

B. Reading

Solar Powered Cars

Solar cars have been developed in the last twenty years and are powered by energy from the sun. Although they are not a practical or economic form of transportation at present, in the future they may play a part in reducing our reliance on burning fossil fuels such as petrol and diesel.

A solar powered racing car (Figure 7-12) is shown above. These are expensive to produce and usually seat only one or two people. The main cost is due to the large number of expensive and delicate photovoltaic solar panels that are needed to power the vehicle. Also, many of the solar powered cars used in races today are composed of expensive, lightweight materials such as titanium composites. These materials are normally used to manu-

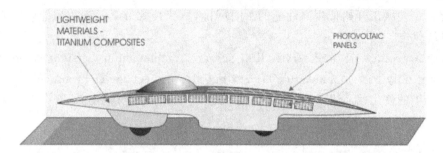

Figure 7-12 Solar powered racing car

facture fighter jets. Carbon fibre and fibre glass are also used for much of the bodywork. Most of the cars used in races are hand made by specialist teams and this adds to the expense.

A solar powered vehicle (Figure 7-13) can only run efficiently when the sun shines, although most vehicles of this type have a battery backup. Electricity is stored in the batteries when the sun is shining and this power can be used when sun light is restricted (cloudy). The batteries are normally nickel-metal hydride batteries (NiMH), Nickel-Cadmium batteries (NiCd), Lithium ion batteries or Lithium polymer batteries. Common lead acid batteries of the type used in the average family car are too heavy. Solar powered cars normally operate in a range of 80 to 170 volts. To reduce friction with the ground the wheels are extremely narrow and there are usually only three.

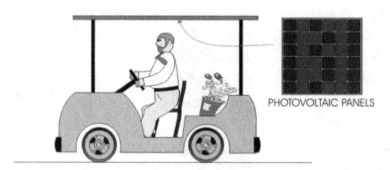

Figure 7-13 A solar powered vehicle

Some solar powered cars are practical and one is shown below. This is a solar powered golf cart and it can be used in sunny climates to carry golfers from one hole to the next. When it is standing still the solar panels charge up the batteries and it is the batteries that power the electric motors, directly. As the vehicle is not in continuous use the batteries have time to charge up before they are needed.

One of the more realistic ways in which the solar powered cars could become practical is to charge up their batteries when they are parked, during the day. Imagine driving the short distance to work and plugging the car into a set of photovoltaic solar panels. Whilst you are working, the batteries charge up ready for use for the journey home. The same procedure could be carried out when the car is parked at home. A combination of solar power and wind power may prove to be a method of charging the batteries of "electric cars".

New Words and Expressions

transportation [ˌtrænspɔːˈteiʃn]	n. 交通运输
delicate [ˈdelikət]	adj. 精致的
racing car	赛车
fighter jet	战斗机
plug into	插入，接通，收听

Technical Terms

titanium composites	钛基复合材料
carbon fibre	碳纤维
nickel-metal hydride battery	镍金属氢化物电池
nickel-cadmium battery	镉镍电池
lithium ion battery	锂离子电池
lithium polymer battery	锂聚合物电池

Notes

1. Although they are not a practical or economic form of transportation at present, in the future they may play a part in reducing our reliance on burning fossil fuels such as petrol and diesel.

虽然目前它们不是一个可行的或经济的运输方式，但在未来它们可能在减少我们对化石燃料如汽油和柴油的依赖中扮演一定角色。

2. A solar powered vehicle can only run efficiently when the sun shines, although most vehicles of this type have a battery backup.

虽然大多数这种类型的车辆有一个备用电池，但是太阳能汽车只能在阳光普照时有效地运行。

3. One of the more realistic ways in which the solar powered cars could become practical is to charge up their batteries when they are parked, during the day.

一个更现实的方式是在白天停着时，太阳能汽车充电，这样它就能变得实用。

4. A combination of solar power and wind power may prove to be a method of charging the batteries of "electric cars".

将太阳能和风能相结合可能被证明是一种给电动汽车充电的方法。

Unit 4

A. Text

Pros and Cons of CHP

1. CHP

Combined heat and power (CHP), or co-generation, is the simultaneous generation of electricity and heat. Tri-generation is a further extension to include a refrigeration process for air conditioning as well.

(1) Conventional electricity generation

Many electricity generation processes make use of a heat engine. The efficiency of the heat engine depends on the ratio of the input heat of the working fluid to the output heat. This typically requires a form of heat exchanger to transfer heat into a cooling fluid i.e. water or air. Due to the relatively low efficiency of most heat engines, the energy available in this cooling fluid may be two or more times as much as in the electricity generated. This heat energy in most conventional power stations is simply dissipated to air and/or river or sea water, in cooling towers.

(2) Applications of CHP

• CHP is most suitable when there is year round demand for heat to balance the demand for electricity, but is useful

• When there is a requirement for space heating or process heat close to the generator

• To provide low temperature (up to 90℃) hot water heating for local district schemes

• For applications that require (low grade) process heat, especially those that can supply their own fuel (i.e. sawmills and wood process industry which use heat for timber drying and steaming)

• At sites such as hospitals, leisure centres, greenhouses, and retirement complexes which have a year round heat demand

• To provide steam for other industrial applications

• Where there is a requirement for environmentally responsible disposal of waste (i.e. sewage sludge, clinical waste or agricultural residue) and where transport costs for disposal are high

• To power an absorption refrigerator to provide cooling in summer, giving tri-generation.

2. Pros

High electricity prices and the high "carbon intensity" of UK pool electricity provide powerful economic and environmental arguments for using biomass to generate electricity.

These arguments are further strengthened if heat produced during electricity production is used to heat buildings or channeled into industrial processes rather than being dumped to the atmosphere with exhaust gases. Using heat in this way can increase efficiency of the power generation system from around 20% or less to over 80%.

3. Cons

Generally small scale thermal electricity generation has low efficiency compared to large scale generation.

Novel generation technologies for small scale thermal electricity generation are being developed but conversion efficiencies remain low compared to heat only applications. There needs to be a valid use for the heat produced during electricity generation and consideration given to what this will be during summer months when heat demand may be lower.

Using the heat to drive an absorption chiller to provide cooling when heat is not required has been pursued by some manufacturers.

An alternative approach is to generate electricity only when there is sufficient demand for heat, and use electricity from alternative sources at other times. However, this may extend financial payback times for the installation.

Future developments

Many of the technologies for small scale (<1MWe) biomass CHP are still under development, and while some case studies show reliable long term operation others may have shown promise on the lab bench but may be more appropriately considered as being at the demonstration or pilot stage at present.

This is an area of considerable development and progress is constantly being made.

New Words and Expressions

dissipate ['disipeit]	v. 耗散
timber ['timbə(r)]	n. 木材
chiller ['tʃilə]	n. 冷水机组
absorption refrigerator	吸收式制冷机
lab bench	实验室工作台

Technical Terms

combined heat and power	热电联供
conventional electricity generation	常规发电
sewage sludge	污水污泥
clinical waste	临床废物
agricultural residue	农业残留物
carbon intensity	碳排放强度

Notes

1. combined heat and power 又称 Co-Generation 指热电联供，也叫做热电联产。是指热力发电厂通过一定的方法，在向用户输出电能的同时，也向用户输出热能。热电联产可以大大提高热电厂的热效率。

2. Tri-generation is a further extension to include a refrigeration process for air conditioning as well.
第三代产品是包括空调制冷过程的进一步扩展。

3. Due to the relatively low efficiency of most heat engines, the energy available in this cooling fluid may be two or more times as much as in the electricity generated.
由于大多数的热机效率相对较低，在该冷却液中可用的能量却是其产生电量的两倍或者更多倍。

4. These arguments are further strengthened if heat produced during electricity production is used to heat buildings or channeled into industrial processes rather than being dumped to the atmosphere with exhaust gases.
在电力生产中产生的热量不再与废气一起倾销到空气中，至于是用于建筑供热还是用于工业过程，争论愈演愈烈。

5. There needs to be a valid use for the heat produced during electricity generation and consideration given to what this will be during summer months when heat demand may be lower.
需要有效的使用发电过程所产生的热，并对在夏季对热能要求较低时的情况进行考虑。

1. Put the following phrases into English:
① 热电联供 ② 污水污泥 ③ 耗散 ④ 实验室工作台
⑤ 农业残留物 ⑥ 碳排放强度 ⑦ 发动机 ⑧ 常规发电

2. Translate the following sentences:
① This typically requires a form of heat exchanger to transfer heat into a cooling fluid i. e. water or air. Due to the relatively low efficiency of most heat engines, the energy available in this cooling fluid may be two or more times as much as in the electricity generated.

② Novel generation technologies for small scale thermal electricity generation are being developed but conversion efficiencies remain low compared to heat only applications.

③ Many of the technologies for small scale (<1MWe) biomass CHP are still under development, and while some case studies show reliable long term operation others may have shown promise on the lab bench but may be more appropriately considered as being at the demonstration or pilot stage at present.

B. Reading

Geothermal Place in the U. S. Power Grid

As states like California move forward with more aggressive Renewable Portfolio Standards (RPS) and seek to reduce greenhouse gas emissions (Figure 7-14), state officials need to consider the full value of the power sources they use, which is critical to ensure that consumers get the most affordable overall system cost and recognize the different reasons for choosing clean power sources.

Figure 7-14 The United States Navy's Coso Geothermal Powerplant in the Mojave Desert at the China Lake Navy Base, California

The California PUC recently noted active questions before policy makers in California and elsewhere, specifically: How to increase amounts of intermittent generation which are impacting grid reliability, to quantify the impact and benefits of various resources to integrate intermittent generation, and what new policies should be adopted to manage the changing electric grid?

These questions are gaining in importance as the United States expands its renewable power production, which today means generating approximately 14 percent of the electricity nationwide. Much of this is coming from wind and solar photovoltaic technologies that rely heavily on the prevailing weather conditions in order to generate power.

New research from the Geothermal Energy Association (GEA) and Geothermal Resources Council (GRC) looks at geothermal as an alternative to intermittent renewable resources.

"Geothermal power offers both firm and flexible solutions to the changing U. S. power system by providing a range of services including but not limited to baseload, regulation, load following or energy imbalance, spinning reserve, non-spinning reserve, and replacement or supplemental reserve." according to the research. The report contends that geothermal power production represents predictable output and long-lasting resources that quickly adjust to fit the needs set by variable renewable energy technologies.

"Having no reliance upon transitory environmental states such as wind and sunlight, geothermal facilities can produce electricity 24 hours a day, 7 days a week," the report says, "As a result, geothermal power plants have a high capacity factor, demonstrating a level of consistency not found in other sources."

The Energy Information Administration (EIA) reports that geothermal power has the highest capacity factor (92 percent) and uses existing transmission capacity efficiently because of its high capacity factor—higher than coal (85 percent), gas (87 percent), or biomass (83 percent). For comparison's sake, the capacity factors for wind (34 percent), solar (20 percent) and solar PV (25 percent).

The retirement of coal plants will provide opportunities for geothermal power plant, which the report says represents the smallest carbon footprint and significantly lower CO_2 emissions than coal or natural gas. The EIA estimates the average levelized cost for geothermal power at $89.60/MWh, slightly lower than coal, nuclear or biomass.

New Words and Expressions

aggressive [ə'gresiv]	adj.	积极行动的
intermittent [ˌintə'mitənt]	adj.	间歇的
baseload ['beisləʊd]	n.	基本负荷
regulation [ˌregju'leiʃn]	n.	调节
transitory ['trænsətri]	adj.	短暂的
comparison [kəm'pærisn]	n.	比较
Geothermal Energy Association		（美国）地热能源协会
Geothermal Resources Council		（美国）地热资源委员会
Energy Information Administration		（美国）能源情报署

Technical Terms

electric grid	电网
load following	负荷跟踪
spinning reserve	旋转备用
supplemental reserve	补充储备
geothermal facility	地热设施

Notes

1. These questions are gaining in importance as the United States expands its renewable power production, which today means generating approximately 14 percent of the electricity nationwide.

当美国扩大可再生能源时，这些问题变得越来越重要。现如今，这就意味着要多产生约百分之十四的全国电力。

2. "Geothermal power offers both firm and flexible solutions to the changing U.S. power system by providing a range of services including but not limited to baseload, regulation, load following or energy imbalance, spinning reserve, non-spinning reserve, and replacement or supplemental reserve." according to the research.

根据研究显示：地热发电通过提供一系列包括不限基本负荷、调节、负荷跟踪或者能量不平衡、旋转备用、非旋转备用、替换或补充储备等服务，以提供既坚实又灵活的解决方案来改变美国的电力系统。

3. For comparison's sake, the capacity factors for wind (34 percent), solar (20 percent) and solar PV (25 percent).

相比之下，风能的利用率是34%，太阳是20%，光伏是25%。

4. The retirement of coal plants will provide opportunities for geothermal power plant, which the report says represents the smallest carbon footprint and significantly lower CO_2 emissions than coal or natural gas.

该报告说，燃煤电厂的弃用将给地热发电厂提供机会，这意味着最小的碳排放和比煤或天然气显著降低的二氧化碳排放量。

References

[1] PV/Wind Grid connected inverter [Z] 2009, Nanjing first second power equipment CO. LTD.

[2] S. R. Wenham, C. B. Honsberg, J. E. Cotter, R. Largent, A. G. Aberle, M. A. Green. Australian Educational and Research Opportunitiesarising through Rapid Growth in the Photovoltaicindustry. Solar Energy Materials&Solar Cells, 2001, 67 (1): 647-654.

[3] Cheng, L & Zhu, T & Liu, Z 2010, New Energy Vehicles will spread in people soon, Sohu, viewed 25 Oct 2010, 〈http://auto.sohu.com/20101018/n275883377.shtml〉.

[4] European Photovoltaic Industry Association (EPIA). Solar Photovoltaic Electricity Empowering the World [R]. Brussels: EPIA, 2011.

[5] European Union Euro server. Pho to voltaic Barometer2010 [R]. Brussels: EU, 2010.

[6] Patrina Eiffert, Ph. D, Gregory J. Kiss. Building-Integrated Photovoltaic Designs for Commercial and Institutional Structures: A Sourcebook for Architects [M]. New York, USA: the Department of Energy's (DOE's) Office of Power Technologies, Photovoltaics Division, and the Federal Energy Management Program. 1999.

[7] J. F. Manwell, L. G. McGowan and A. L. Rogers. Wind energy explained [M]. Amherst, USA: John-wiley & Sons, LTD, 2002.

[8] Baffins. Lane, Wind energy handbook [M]. Chichester, England: John—wiley & Sons, Ltd, 2001.

[9] L. G. Gonzalez et al. Dynamic response analysis of small wind energy conversion systems operating with torque control versus speed control [J]. International Conference on Renewable Energies and Power Quality, 2009.

[10] Manfred Stieler. Wind energy systems for electric power [M]. Berlin, Germany: Springer-Verlag, 2008.

[11] German Wind Energy Association. Hybrid tower prewail [N]. Berlin, Germany: Wind energy market. 2012.

[12] Sathyajith Mathew. Advances in wind energy conversion technology [M]. Kerala, India: Springer-Verlag, 2011.

[13] Zhu Rong et al. Assessment of wind energy potential in China. Beijing, China: Center for Wind and Solar Energy Resources Assessment, 2009.

[14] Donald L. Klass. Biomass forenewable energy and fuels [R]. Barrington, Illinois, United States: Entech Interational, Inc. 2004.

[15] Vaughn Nelson. Wind energy—renewable energy and the environment [M]. London, England: CRC Press, 2009.

[16] Thomas Ackermann. Wind power in power systems [M]. Chichester, England: John-wiley & Sons, Ltd, 2005.

[17] Fthenakis and Alsema (2006), Photovoltaics Energy Payback Times, Greenhouse Gas Emissions and External Costs, 2004-early 2005 Status, V. Fthenakis and E. Alsema, Progress in Photovoltaics: Research and Applications, vol. 14, 2006, p. 275-280.

[18] Prof Nicola Pearsall. Module-SPG8017 Introduction to Bioenergy and Photovoltaics [M]. Newcastle, England: renewable energy enterprise and management, 2006.

[19] [澳]伟纳姆等编,狄大卫等译. 应用光伏学 [M]. 上海:上海交通大学出版社,2009.

[20] 曾盛. 高速公路太阳能供电和风力供电技术应用 [J]. 广东:交通科技与经济. 2008.

[21] 李俊峰等. 中国风电发展报告 [R]. 海南:海南出版社,2010.

[22] 郭连贵. 光伏专业英语 [M]. 北京:化学工业出版社,2012.

[23] 梁昌鑫. 国内外风电的现状和发展趋势 [J]. 上海:上海电机学院学报,2009.